Facts

Interpretations

series editor: Roy Harris

This new series aims to explore the key concepts of intellectual enquiry in the Western world. Some of these concepts have a long and controversial history; others are of relatively recent origin. All are open to different interpretations by different thinkers.

Interpretations has two main aims:

to offer a survey of the main interpretations of an idea: those interpretations which have been influential in the history of Western thought

to offer experts an opportunity to present their own interpretation both of the idea and of its historical importance.

While giving the student an introduction to an important topic in the history of ideas, each volume in the series also represents an original contribution to that subject by a specialist in the field.

The language of the series is that of the general reader. All unfamiliar or technical terms are fully explained and critically evaluated.

Facts

Bede Rundle

Duckworth

First published in 1993 by
Gerald Duckworth & Co. Ltd.
The Old Piano Factory
48 Hoxton Square, London N1 6PB
Tel: 071 729 5986
Fax: 071 729 0015

Distributed in USA by
Focus Information Group
PO Box 369
Newburyport, MA 01950

A catalogue record for this book is available
from the British Library

ISBN 0 7156 2467 9

Typeset by Ray Davies
Printed in Great Britain by
Redwood Press Limited, Melksham

Contents

For Matthew

Preface

Facts are commonly valued above opinions, conjectures, or the products of fiction or fantasy. It is the facts which have the last say, however inspired the conjectures; it is the facts which furnish the rock on which theories, however grand, may founder. But ours is not an age of certainties. Whether for reasons of relativism, pragmatism, or just plain scepticism, the range of what can be established as fact is often held to be far less extensive than we should ordinarily suppose. It is even questioned whether there are such things; certainly, it has been doubted whether *fact* provides the basis for a well-defined and fruitful contrast. One of our concerns will be to defend the utility of the concept against such doubts.

We begin by developing an account of facts which depends on rejecting an assumption which, while widespread and natural, is one of the main sources of their seemingly perplexing character. Arguments aimed at casting doubt on ostensible factual knowledge are then examined and likewise found to be misconceived. Their proponents would have been better advised to take a very different direction, setting their sights on the more realistic goal of proposing alternative concepts rather than overturning obvious truths.

Some of these obvious truths concern matters of value, despite the common contention that values and facts stand opposed. The frequent inconclusiveness of moral debates may appear to testify to their opposition, but we find that the existence of disagreement can be explained without our having to suppose that matters of value cannot at the same time be reckoned matters of fact. On the other hand, this is an area where the possibility of alternative concepts is worth exploring, given the questionable presuppositions which may underlie the concepts used in the disputed judgments.

Large areas of debate open up with these topics, and we can do little more than draw attention to some of the main issues and sketch an approach to them. The approach in question is one which locates a concern with linguistic detail within a broader perspective owing much to Wittgenstein; roughly speaking, we tackle questions of grammar right across a spectrum having at one end grammar as normally understood, and at the other end general conceptual questions to which grammar in the extended sense associated with Wittgenstein applies. Some of the arguments will no doubt be found wanting, but I hope that enough is found persuasive to serve as an advertisement for a way of addressing philosophical problems which, given the nature of the subject, seems to me inescapable, but which too often takes second place to the preoccupation with theory which is one of the major targets of our criticism.

Trinity College, Oxford   B.R.
January 1993

1

The Nature of Facts

What are facts? It is easy enough to provide specimens: it is a fact that the first motor race was from Paris to Rouen and back in 1894, that slavery is still practised in parts of the world today, that angling is the most popular sport in Britain. But what, in general terms, does something have to be to earn a place in this list?

If we look at the various categories which have some affinity with that of facts, we come upon such notions as those of a state of affairs, an event, a truth, or a certainty. Broadly speaking, we have categories which take us outside language, and categories which keep us within. One or other of these domains, surely, will be where facts have their home, so let us consider the two possibilities in turn.

First, does the world deliver what we seek? For Russell, facts are naturally set against beliefs, being what they are whatever we may choose to think about them, whereas beliefs are either true or false by reference to facts. That the world contains facts is, says Russell, a truism. He does not propose to offer an exact definition, but a fact can be explained as the kind of thing which makes a proposition true or false.[1]

The account of truth to which Russell is subscribing – the 'correspondence theory' – may strike us as little more than a platitude: the truth of a statement or proposition surely depends on something outside thought and language; it is not a matter of what is said being in agreement with something else we or another might say or believe, but at some point we must exit from language, and facts, says the theory, are what we encounter on exit.

What form does this correspondence or agreement take? It is held that a proposition, *p*, is true if and only if, first, it is a fact that *p*, and second, the proposition corresponds to that fact. Clearly, however, the second clause adds nothing to the first: for *p* to be true it is enough that it should be a fact that *p*. Or, if any correspondence is involved, it is only in the weak sense that this implies – that for any true proposition there should be an associated fact. Still, this is no real objection. The simplified equivalence, '*p* is true if and only if it is a fact that *p*', retains the significance of the original so long as the conditions thus paired relate to language and the world respectively, and the superfluity of the second clause simply absolves us from having to make sense of any more complex relation – one, for instance, in which the proposition is somehow to mirror its fact in a point-by-point fashion.

But if there is any substance to the claim that facts are in the world, it should be possible to justify this 'in', to say *where* they are to be found, yet there appears to be no answer to such a question as 'Where is the fact that inflation has fallen?' We can ask where, in what countries, it is a fact that inflation has fallen, but not where in those countries that fact is to be found. For worldly items facts are peculiarly elusive, being undetectable by any of the senses or by any scientific instrument. And peculiarly insubstantial: they cannot be weighed, measured, dissected or destroyed; they do not compete for space with anything, are quite incapable of acting upon such undeniably concrete things as sticks and stones. Might facts then be events or happenings? These, after all, are likewise lacking in substance. An event may indeed be a fact, in the sense that it may be a fact that such-and-such an event took place, but the terms that complete '... is a fact' into a sentence cannot be counted on to perform the same service for '... is an event'. That the moon is devoid of life may be a fact, it is certainly not an event; a fact may be stated, contested or conceded, not so an event. Conversely, while an event may occur or take place, and take place at some location, that is not the lot of a fact. Again, if Voltaire died peacefully, then 'Voltaire's death' and 'Voltaire's peaceful death' pick out the same event, but the fact that Voltaire died is not the same fact as the fact that he died peacefully. Someone may, for instance, have learned of the former while remaining ignorant of the latter.

Are facts then states of affairs? With respect to, say, 'It is a fact that the elephant is the largest land mammal', the notion of a state of affairs is less inapposite than that of an event, but again there is no question of interchanging the two phrases. States of affairs compare with events and contrast with facts in having a beginning and going on for a certain time; you can be involved in and try to change a state of affairs, unlike a fact; conversely, a fact can be challenged or disputed, unlike a state of affairs.

Are facts then to be found in language? This undoubtedly looks more promising. Someone who asks for the facts hopes to be presented with a number of true propositions or statements; facts, like truths, may be accepted, challenged, or denied; a matter of fact is opposed to a matter of conjecture, a mere supposition or hypothesis. However, to treat 'fact' as a predicate of linguistic items soon brings its own incongruities. Overlooking or distorting a fact is perhaps a matter of overlooking or distorting a true proposition, but there is no simple equation of 'fact' with 'true proposition'. Propositions may be in English, contain terms referring to persons and things, be ambiguous, be uttered or expressed, mistranslated or misattributed, not so facts. Most simply, a true proposition is a proposition, a fact is not.

But if facts are neither in language nor in the world, what is left for them? One radical possibility is this: the phrase 'is a fact' *is not true of anything whatsoever*. This would explain in the most decisive fashion why each of these attempts to pin facts down has come to nothing, the expression being impossible to anchor, either to anything within language or to anything outside it. Perhaps we are mesmerised by a false picture: we see a role for 'fact' only in conveying what sort of thing something is, when its actual behaviour belies its surface grammar. You say it is a fact that plants release oxygen, but is there anything whose *kind* you are specifying? Surely, what you say is more by way of an emphatic affirmation rather than a description of an item identified by the clause, 'that plants release oxygen'.

If 'fact' fails to be true of anything, is this to say that there are no such things as facts? For the early Wittgenstein the world was the totality of facts, but set beside the things which we should first think of as worldly items, facts might be deemed to be no things at all. Indeed, it may seem that we have shown as much. However, usage of the term 'thing' can be so undemanding, it may represent no concession on anyone's part to grant that there are such things. If it is true, for instance, that the jury considered all the relevant facts in reaching its verdict, then the general denial that there are facts is simply untenable. Again, while saying it is a fact that *p* is a matter of stating rather than describing, it is not true that we can never be said to describe a fact; we do just that when we say that such-and-such a fact is important, or difficult to grasp. On the other hand, it is of some significance that we do not so readily speak of facts as *existing*. What we do say is that it is a fact that such-and-such. It is a fact that Scott reached the South Pole, that a form of plastic was produced as far back as 1855. If we can get clear on what this central context involves we should be clear about the nature of our quarry. Compare the term 'event'. Events are not the sorts of thing that are naturally said to exist; rather, they take place or come about. But of course there *are* events – things happen – and equally there are facts – I have just stated two.

Among the things said to be facts we can number events, episodes and states, but it may be wondered how this can be so if 'fact' is not to be considered true of anything. These ways of speaking are not them-selves in question, but it is a certain way of construing them that is to be rejected, namely, when it is suppos-edly a matter of categorising something referred to. Philosophers and logicians attach great importance to the form of sentence in which one term, the subject, serves to identify or refer to something of which the remainder of the sentence, the predicate, is affirmed. An insistence on discerning the subject-predicate pat-tern in the types of sentence which concern us is one source of perplexity with regard to facts, and we might ask whether there really is much to be said for a parsing of 'That *p* is a fact' which would make it out to be like 'The desk is an antique', say, in respect of anything beyond its superficial grammatical form. A noun clause is surely a most implausible contender for the role of referring to something.

Take 'It is a fact that William III died in 1702'. What is here being said to be a fact is a certain event or episode, but it is a matter of declaring some historical event to be a fact rather than saying *of* some event that it is a fact. It is, we might say, a matter of the words of the clause serving merely to *specify* a certain event, not actually to name or refer to one – the use needed for 'fact' to be true of something. Compare such a remark as 'A screwdriver would be useful'. The speaker need not be referring to an actual screwdriver and affirming something of it, but here too we may say that he is specifying or stating what would be useful. Again, while an episode can be a fact, if it is said, 'There was an ugly episode. He failed to take this fact into account', it is not a matter of redescribing the episode as a fact, but the fact in question is that there was an ugly episode. Similarly, from 'It is a fact that the market is depressed' we can infer 'The depressed state of the market is a fact', but 'is a fact' continues to shun a role in which it would predicate something of the state, the appropriate elucidation again being furnished by a clausal rendering: 'That the market is in a depressed state is a fact.' Finally, my refusal to allow that facts can act upon anything would be challenged by those who think of causes as facts, but this could be true only in the sense that it may be a fact that such-and-such is a cause. It is nonsense to say that, for example, a fact caused a person's injuries.

Someone might object: I can understand why the

noun clause should be denied a referential role both in 'It is a fact that *p*' and 'It is not a fact that *p*'. The reasons are much as with the denial that the grammatical subject of an existential statement is a logical subject, i.e. one used to refer to something. So, if *A* says, 'It is a fact that carrots are good for the eyes', whereas *B* insists, 'That is just a popular misconception', then the same thing is being said to be, or not to be, a fact, and if *B* is right, then it can hardly be something in the world that is being judged. However, suppose *A* is right. Once granted the fact in question, why should we not then refer to it as to a worldly item? Surely, after all, a full inventory of the world would have to extend to the relations which hold between things as well as to the things themselves, relations which constitute facts about things.

There is no doubt that we can refer to facts, as when we say that the facts we have gathered suggest a hypothesis, but since the clause which occurs in apposition to 'fact' can also occur in apposition to a term such as 'conjecture', it is difficult to see how it could ever be suited to singling out a worldly item. True, there are other grammatical subjects, more promising than clauses, which are capable of designating events or acts, as well as merely specifying them: along with 'His fall is a fact' we also have 'His fall was painful'. However, not only does the former ring awkwardly, but the appropriateness of the clausal rendering, 'That he fell is a fact', again points to a different behaviour on the part of the subject. The noun phrases which can join with 'is a fact' to form a sentence, and which more readily submit to the latter paraphrase, are those whose use more generally reveals them as doing duty for clauses. So, 'The existence of quarks is a fact' is natural enough, and the clausal role is apparent in many other contexts: 'He questioned the existence of quarks (whether quarks exist)', 'He demonstrated the existence of quarks (that quarks exist)', and so forth.

To counter the idea that 'fact' can do what we ask of it only if it can be true of something, we may point to the near equivalence of, e.g., 'It is a fact that she has recovered' with 'She has in fact recovered', where the contribution of 'fact' is now channelled through an adverbial phrase. This illustrates a familiar choice: we say indifferently 'It appears that the summers are getting hotter' or 'The summers are apparently getting hotter'; along with 'It is possible that the summers are getting hotter' we find both 'The summers are possibly getting hotter' and 'The summers may be getting hotter', the qualification being one which can equally be conveyed by a modal verb or adverb. Likewise for 'It is a fact that A is F' with its corresponding forms, 'A is in fact F' and 'A is actually F'. Even when, as with 'possible', we have a term which it makes sense to attach to a proposition, there is no necessity to think of the adjective as predicated of the noun clause. There is not a single pattern here, but with 'fact', and the terms with which it compares, we are introducing a qualification into the mode of affirmation, giving a further determination of its character rather than drawing attention to a feature that is true of the clause or of something this designates.

If this approach is correct, 'It is a fact that p' is best understood, not as a predication, but as a co-ordination of the two clauses which it comprises, so as: 'It is a fact: p', or 'A fact: p', the 'it' being a mere dummy pronoun rather than a stand-in for what follows. Compare 'It is a miracle that they survived', or 'It is only natural that he should feel aggrieved'. Traditionally, the pronoun 'it' would be thought of as an anticipatory subject for the subject proper, the latter seemingly coming with the clause and presenting us with a propositional term, but there is no question of a proposition's being a miracle, or only natural. True, there is *a* sense in which a proposition may be said to be a fact, but it is one in line with our reading of 'It is a fact that p'; that is, it is not a matter of saying what sort of thing the proposition is. This is in no sense to deny that, if it is a fact that p, then something is indeed a fact; it is, once more, merely to refuse a certain construal of these words. Compare the inference from 'Why he did it is clear' to 'Something is clear'. The term 'something' is trivially allowable in lieu of the clause; its introduction does not require that the clause supplanted should *designate* something – which it plainly does not – nor that the clause itself should be what is affirmed to be clear. For one who seeks illumination as to what precisely is being said to be clear, it is to no avail to reiterate the given clause, 'why he did it', let alone the bare 'something', but we should look beyond the immediate grammatical form to a more perspicuous expansion: what is being said to be clear is the answer to the question, 'Why did he do it?'. Likewise with 'Something is a fact', allowance made for the different type of clause.

It would, however, be going too far to say that every use of the term 'fact' can be handled along the lines proposed. The word frequently enters into figurative uses – facts are hard or stubborn; we speak of facing the facts, of the facts as speaking for themselves. There is no expectation that we should be able to give a systematic account of such uses; on the contrary, the involvement of metaphor makes that most unlikely. It may even be that 'fact' should come to attach itself to what are undeniably identifications of worldly items; it is just that this would be a departure from the use revealed in the standard locutions considered. Here we may note that such forms as 'High prices are a fact' are to be understood along the pattern suggested: not 'High prices are facts', as though we were saying what sort of thing they were, but 'It is a fact that prices are high', or 'Prices are in fact high'. We may also note that a statement of a negative fact poses no problem: 'That fairies do not exist is a fact' says no more than 'Fairies do not in fact exist'.

*

Although we have rejected any simple equation of 'fact' with 'true proposition', this comes closer to the truth than does a construal which would place facts in the world, and it might be that a more roundabout equivalence between these two notions remains a possibility. That is, without holding that the one phrase could simply replace the other, the suggestion is that anything said making use of 'fact' could be expressed by rephrasing the context with the help of 'true proposition'.

However, this seems to be so only when what is contributed by 'fact' is smuggled into the formulation with 'true' through some *additional* term. For instance, *ascertaining* that p is true may be a matter of *ascertaining* that it is a fact that p. More generally, however, 'true' enjoys a broader application. For instance, we are permitted to *suppose* that p may be true without supposing it to be a fact that p, the latter being so only when *p* can be reckoned among *known* truths. Granted, we sometimes speak as if facts were facts independently of anything known – 'We do not as yet have all the facts' – but it would seem that the requisite knowledge is then anticipated. It is not here implied that there are certain things which are a matter of fact at the time of speaking but of which we are not as yet apprised. At the time of speaking they may be only conjecture.

Certainly, the characterisation, 'Facts are what true statements state', is not adequate to capturing what is distinctive of 'fact', but we need to enlist the condition of being settled or established, the contrast with conjecture or opinion being as important as that with falsity. It is a fact: uncle has been declared bankrupt. It is not a question of a possibility we can still take steps to avert; not a matter of speculation, of something there is any point in trying to cast doubt upon; it is vain to hope that there has been a mistake, that it is only appearance. The term is not just an intensifier, but it retains something of its etymology, a lingering remnant of the idea of something *done*, something unalterably fixed. Compare 'deed' and the close relation of 'in fact' given by 'indeed'.

However, while 'unknown facts' may have an awkward ring, it is perhaps no less awkward to say that, for instance, when Socrates was alive it was not a fact that the world was round. Not a fact for Socrates and his contemporaries, perhaps, but to say not a fact *sans phrase* suggests we are denying that the world was then round. It is indeed awkward to speak in this way, but the unwanted reading does not necessarily impose itself. We can happily say, 'As I speak, it is not a fact that there is life on other planets', while not ruling out the possibility that somewhere there is extra-terrestrial life waiting to be discovered.

Or so I should say. Others may feel that the connexion with knowledge is being overstated, that 'fact' need carry no more implications in this regard than does 'true'. I should wish to insist that a use in which the idea of being settled or established is central has to be acknowledged, but I grant that little is made of this implication in many contexts. Think, for instance, of the frequent (and unlovely) use of the term to provide a bridge between a phrase and a clause which the former cannot govern directly, as with 'Due to the fact that ...' and 'Despite the fact that ...'. With 'He finished the meal despite the fact that he felt unwell', the implication of unquestionable knowledge is hardly to the fore, but we should probably be happy to settle for 'He finished the meal despite feeling unwell' in its stead. There is a similar use of 'fact' as a subject of such verbal phrases as 'means', 'shows', and 'makes it likely'. Here 'makes true' is of interest for its possible appearance in the correspondence theory of truth. It can rightly be said that the fact that fairies do not exist makes 'Fairies do not exist' true. Such 'making' is, of course, not causal, any more than it is in 'He is my sister's son; that makes him my nephew', but in both cases the relation is 'grammatical', in Wittgenstein's sense — to the disadvantage of the correspondence theory, should it look to this idiom to find its elusive extralinguistic relation.

It is clear more generally that the correspondence theory cannot profit from an appeal to facts. In those cases where it is a matter of known truth, what can be said in such terms can indeed be restated in terms of facts, but while, say, ascertaining that *p* is true is just ascertaining that it is a fact that *p*, there is no question of the fact side of the equation taking us to a complementary worldly item. Moreover, if I am right in my claim that truth is in general wider than factual character, there will be instances of true propositions where the second term of the correspondence relation is lacking altogether.

In losing the correspondence theory it may be felt that we lose more than we should wish. Surely truth requires *some* form of correspondence between words and world? There is no denying that we make contact with the world with words, in the sense of referring in various ways to persons, places and things. What is to be rejected is the idea of a relation over and above any relation that the proposition in question might present as a matter of its own internal structure. I mean: suppose it is said that 'Soot is black' presents us with a species of predicative relation – 'is black' is predicated of what is named by 'soot'. Then, of course, the proposition is true if and only if the relation holds; that is, if and only if soot – something likely to be found in the world – *is* black. Anything the supposed relation of correspondence might achieve has already been provided for without going beyond the relation which the proposition itself incorporates – and without singling out a bogus complex which is to answer to the verbal form as a whole.

We have seen that 'fact' does not equate, either directly or indirectly, with 'true proposition'. Adding the qualification 'known' or 'established' still does not give us a direct equivalence, though it may be that some such formula offers a means for re-expressing, in a more roundabout fashion, anything sayable with 'fact'. However that may be, the consideration of prime importance is that in stating that such-and-such is a fact we are not describing anything, whether in language or in the world. Our task is not to make sense of some unfathomable entity, but in so far as there is a problem it is one of knowing when we are entitled to proclaim something a fact. We shall consider some aspects of this question in the next chapter.

2

Fact and Theory

Fact is opposed to fiction and fantasy; it is also opposed to hypothesis, conjecture and theory. Each of these contrasts is of interest to philosophy, but the one which takes us closest to the heart of current concerns is that between fact and theory, the ascendancy of theory, often at the expense of fact, being a distinctive feature of much contemporary philosophy.

The roots of this development are to be found in a dissatisfaction with the limited, largely critical, ambitions of earlier analytical philosophy, coupled with a belief that features which are the hallmark of a good scientific hypothesis, features such as generality, simplicity and explanatory adequacy, are equally to be reckoned signs of philosophical rectitude. The scientific approach has penetrated even further into philosophy with the claim that anything from an abstraction to a macroscopic object is appropriately 'posited', much as with the theoretical entities of physics.

What has emerged to date with this scientific turn is, as I see it, little by way of anything that might be called a 'theory', much by way of a distancing from what really matters, a preoccupation with theory tending to divert discussion into 'programmatic' considerations which lead nowhere, but which stand in the way of getting to grips with the real problems. At its worst, we find a diminished concern with the all-important aim of getting things right: plead a concern with theory, and somehow inconvenient counter-examples no longer appear so destructive of one's position. Moreover, for at least one major philosophical task – the exposure of nonsense – we do not *need* a theory. Much analytical philosophy, especially of the ordinary language variety, was liable to degenerate into triviality, but this was a fault of its practitioners rather than of the method generally, which simply aimed at bringing as much rigour and as few preconceptions as possible to the task of achieving clarity and understanding.[2]

One of the excesses of the theory-driven alternative which we shall fasten on relates to the matter of positing or postulating various entities. It should be clear from our analysis that there is no scope for such a procedure with respect to facts themselves. Whether such-and-such is a fact may be difficult to establish, but the difficulty does not lie with the obscure nature of an entity which goes by the name of 'fact', an entity which we can do no better than postulate. Philosophers are sometimes loath to make use of terms which, like 'fact', do not name anything concrete. It would be more in place to welcome them, precisely because their use is so much less demanding than any term for a physical entity. There is, after all, nothing by way of a *constitution* which a fact might have and which we might not know how to make give up its secrets. Again, consider numbers. What do we do to show that there are negative numbers, for instance? We explain the notion of a negative number. This explanation will doubtless proceed with the help of examples, at which point there is nothing lacking which, *faute de mieux*, might have to be introduced as a mere posit. All that has to answer to the notation is an intelligible *use*, not a system of problematic entities.

Here it should be noted that the kind of theory we are dealing with is usually further removed from fact than is customary outside philosophy. To explain, there is a familiar development whereby, starting with a conjecture or hypothesis, we set about gathering data which might establish it more securely. So, for a time, Harvey's theory of the circulation of blood through the body was theory only; with further findings it entered the domain of fact. Again, there are many words whose correct use presupposes happenings beyond the here and now. The word 'father', for instance, applies only if the relevant generative relationship holds. Should this feature be taken to warrant classing 'father' among 'theoretical' terms, this would not mean that statements in which it figured could not aspire to factual status. Once more, theoretical character need mark only a passing phase in the life of a proposition. There may be no precise point at which it is reasonable to regard a hypothesis as having attained factual standing, but there is in general no insuperable obstacle to such attainment. Even a theory as remote from everyday experience as the atomic theory of matter would now be accepted by the scientific world as part of established fact. Certainly, something has gone awry if the domain of theory is allowed to encroach upon that of fact to such a degree that even truths of the most mundane and uncontroversial variety are held to belong ineluctably to the former. As an example of the extremes to which some may go in redrawing the relevant boundaries, consider the following from Karl Popper:

Almost every statement we make transcends experience. There is no sharp dividing line between an 'empirical language' and a 'theoretical language': *we are theorizing all the time*, even when we make the most trivial singular statement.[3]

The source of this unremitting theorizing is located in the supposedly dispositional character of most of our descriptions. Thus, to describe something as 'elastic' is to imply that it will revert to its original shape when a distorting force is removed, but a check for this property would allegedly require investigation of indefinitely many circumstances in which a force might be applied and withdrawn, and that is simply not possible. This character is ubiquitous, extending even to a term such as 'broken':

> If 'breakable' is dispositional, so is 'broken', considering for example how a doctor decides whether a bone is broken or not. Nor should we call a glass 'broken' if the pieces would fuse the moment they were put together: the criterion of being broken is behaviour *under certain conditions*.[4]

Popper would have had a much stronger case with the term 'unbreakable'. For the unbreakability of an object to be anything more than a provisional hypothesis, it would need the support of a view about molecular structure, say, which would enable us to anticipate its success in passing further tests, a view which might well qualify as theory. It is implausible to treat 'breakable' as comparable, and utterly absurd to treat 'broken' this way. If we can as much as speak of the *pieces* of glass as fusing together we are perforce speaking of a *broken* glass, and if they did fuse it would just mean that the glass could no longer be spoken of as broken, not that we had not had to do with a broken glass up to that point. Similarly, given the ease with which we might reassure ourselves that a rubber band, say, is elastic, it is difficult to see what bearing an infinity of possible tests could have on our finding. After all, if, at a certain point, the appropriate behaviour is no longer forthcoming, we have a case of something losing its elasticity, not a proof that it never was elastic. It is simply a misrepresentation of our ascriptions of elasticity, opacity, solidity, and so forth, to construe them as laying claim to truth for all eternity.

Not merely language, but even observation itself has been held to be theory-laden; merely to *see* what the scientist sees we must learn some science: 'the physicist sees an X-ray tube, the child a complicated lamp bulb; the microscopist sees coelenterate mesoglea, his new student sees only a gooey, formless stuff.'[5] But of course the child can be said to see an X-ray tube. He just does not know that that is what it is. True, he does not see *that* it is an X-ray tube, but this way of speaking belongs with what has just been denied, not with what we have affirmed.

*

Our interest is in considerations which would have us move the dividing line between the factual and the theoretical in the direction of the former, or indeed have us eliminate some class of putative facts entirely. One class which would seem well able to resist any moves towards its abolition is that of claims that some physical object or substance has some detectable property. What could be further beyond question than the fact that buttercups are yellow? However, even this class is held to be at risk, coming up, as it does, against two claims: first, that secondary qualities, such as colours and tastes, are subjective, that their ascriptions to objects are accordingly not to be numbered among statements of fact; second, that the material bodies of the familiar macroscopic world are best treated as having the status of merely theoretical entities.

This latter position may be presented as an extension of the view which has been thought vindicated at the submicroscopic level. Physicists have found it enormously profitable to postulate a range of particles below the level of the observable. These entities are accepted, not, it is held, because their existence is a literal truth, but because they are part of a model which offers the simplest account of observed phenomena. The everyday notion of a macroscopic object serves a similar explanatory purpose, it is suggested, though it could in principle be jettisoned in favour of some other concept or concepts. For some, indeed, it has been shown to be inapplicable, the 'abandonment of solid matter' being claimed as one of the triumphs of twentieth-century science.

We could no doubt make use of radically different concepts in describing the world; perhaps, even, there could be languages having no match for our names of material things, like 'tile', 'kettle', or 'peg'. True, we are as yet in the dark about what could serve our purposes better, but granted that physical object terminology might be superseded in some areas for some purposes, that does not make it appropriate to enlist the term 'theory' in connexion with current usage, since the factual character of what is said with the standard vocabulary remains unaffected by the availability of an alternative.

That we might simply abjure conventional material object terminology does not appear to be what is being suggested by those who regard material objects as theoretical entities, but two theses appear to be involved:

(i) a counter to the claim that the existence of material objects is an assured, unshakeable fact.

(ii) the idea that positing them provides us with a means of organising our experience in a systematic fashion.

If it is allowed that physical object concepts are at least usable, that it is *intelligible* to say 'The kettle is on the stove', it becomes puzzling to know why a knowable truth is none the less not in prospect. It is not as if literal truth were precluded through the involvement of figures of speech in the use of such concepts, as may happen with the terms used in a model. Perhaps the most likely reply is that, in so far as a term like 'kettle' has implications as to physical constitution, affirmations in which it figures go beyond the deliverances of the senses.

It might still be wondered whether any theory for which the existence of physical objects is problematic can make sense of that notion. How could the material object hypothesis explain anything to someone who held that experience never presented him with instances of the concept? We can explain a bump in the carpet by supposing that a solid object is lodged under-neath. We can do this because we have learned by experience something of the behaviour of bodies, but if they were only theoretical, there would be no ques-tion of our having the requisite knowledge to draw upon.

The belief that physical objects strictly transcend sense experience appears to be necessary if there is to be room for an explanatory role for them, but at the same time to cast doubt on the intelligibility of such a role. Moreover, for the most part we do not in fact introduce objects in this capacity, our ordinary talk being largely reportive rather than explanatory. Where we do have the latter, this will be only because observation is contingently lacking. Nor do we in fact argue from sensations or sense-data to material exist-ence, but as far as any inferences go, the physical has the status of a starting point, not a conclusion. It would normally pass as quite uncontroversial to judge *di-rectly* of the physical; indeed, perverse to do anything less. There is no question of a rash, hazardous, or flawed procedure, but we are talking about a practice that has stood the test of time as well as any.

But must it not be admitted that in some sense we go beyond the evidence when, for instance, we describe what we see on looking out of the window? Sight, after all, is of things at a distance, and it could conceivably turn out that on going up to the apparent garden gnome we should find that we passed right through it. Certainly, if the description we give is based on noth-ing more than a casual glance, we cannot claim that a more considered examination of our surroundings is bound to leave it unchallenged. Very well, we can be said to 'go beyond the evidence' in this sense: it is consistent with how things seem that subsequent developments should cast doubt on our claim, or even show it to be wrong.[6] This suggestion is not one we need resist – it does not involve the dubious contention that we actually make an *inference* with such claims – but then, in an overwhelming number of cases, the judgment which is said to go beyond the evidence is one that is found to be vindicated: the grey, gnomelike form fully measures up to our expectations of solidity. Furthermore, to the extent that subsequent developments are indicative of error, to that extent they at least are to be accorded a standing as veridical, so there is no question of a wholesale rejection of judgments of the kind in question.

But consider the situation which is thought to deliver more final verification, the situation in which we speak of encountering a solid object. Is this not also an occasion on which, in all strictness, we should speak merely of sensations experienced? Here it can at least be granted that the key term 'sensation' is in order, whereas it has no relevant role with respect to vision, for which the other terms customarily invoked – 'sense-datum', *quale*, 'percept', 'impression' – are also problematic. But the situation remains one where use of our familiar material object terms remains so far unimpugned, one where there are no realistic grounds for doubt about the modest claim made in those terms, the kind of situation in which we might say: this is just what it is to come into contact with a physical object.

Granted there is no cogent way of challenging the propriety of our familar way of speaking, might it not be possible, none the less, to make use of concepts of pure sensation to elaborate an alternative conceptual scheme? Such a scheme has never progressed beyond its proposal, and there are reasons for thinking it unrealisable. We are somehow to say what is customarily formulated in physical object language by making use of terms relating merely to the sensations through which physical objects make known their presence. In this connexion it is crucial that our body has the role it has: it is because we meet with resistance when we press against an object that we know we have to do with something corporeal. Not only is our body thus presupposed, but given that the information extracted from these encounters relates to the physical – is, indeed, information which might be acquired by observing the object in question in interaction with other, non-sentient, bodies – it is difficult to see how the same information could be conveyed in the impoverished sensation language proposed.

However, this difficulty is not my main interest. The notion of positing material things, where this is a matter of supposing them to exist for the sake of simplicity, with no question of a further advance to actual knowledge of their existence, meets with insuperable difficulties through being understood – and being intended to be understood – as a challenge to what we regard as a matter of fact, a denial that we ever strictly see or touch material things. If F is a physical object concept at the homely level of *cup* or *cap*, 'We do not have to admit Fs' is not at all plausible if taken as 'The grounds for acknowledging the existence of Fs are not compelling', but any 'positing' should be at the grammatical level: 'There is an alternative to speaking of Fs.' To grant this does not mean that we cannot speak of *facts* in just the way we do; in countless circumstances there are no grounds for doubting the existence of something physical. There is no philosophical choice *within* the scheme as to what facts there are; that is to be decided in familiar non-philosophical ways. But there may be a choice as to what scheme we shall adopt. Perhaps we can speak in terms of sense-data, perhaps – to take a rather different kind of possibility – we can speak in terms of events; though these are possibilities only in the sense that they are not known to be incoherent.

It may be protested that the claim that material objects cannot be dislodged from the secure position with which common sense credits them is not warranted in the light of modern physics, which has overturned the plain man's conception of solid matter. Not merely are material objects part of what is no more than a theory; it is a theory that is due for replacement. Recall Eddington's table:

> ... there is a vast difference between my scientific table with its substance (if any) thinly scattered in specks in a region mostly empty and the table of everyday conception which we regard as the type of solid reality.[7]

We can go some way towards dispelling the impression of a serious clash with common sense by noting the limited extent to which such a clash must be acknowledged. In some cases it may come as a surprise to find that a liquid can seep through something which displays no readily visible porosity, and we might deem such an object less solid than we had supposed. It also comes as a jolt to our normal conceptions to find that certain physical particles can pass right through chunks of solid matter, but the retreat that either of these happenings obliges us to make does not take us outside the commonsense picture. We have to make an adjustment of our beliefs at their periphery, not abandon them at the centre. However, while this point takes us some distance towards reconciliation, it does not appear to help square this picture with one outstanding consideration, namely the minuscule bulk of the matter in any macroscopic body when set against the (relatively) enormous tracts of space found within the confines of that body.

The source of the conflict here lies, I suggest, in an uncritical adoption of the model commonly used to represent the structure of matter at the atomic level, namely, the model of particles disposed much as bodies in the solar system, but compressed by an astronomically large factor. Macroscopic bodies have surfaces, surfaces which may be rough or smooth, wet or dry, opaque or transparent. There is no guarantee that the features which pass as the norm at this level continue to make sense as attributes of the particles which the solar system model seeks to depict. It would be simple-minded to think of fundamental particles as coming in a range of colours, or as possessed of other sensible qualities; even to speak of a *particle* is not to invoke a category that stands in no need of justification. This is not a purely formal concept, like 'thing', but there are conditions which have to be met before its use can be deemed apposite, and it should not surprise us if those conditions are not invariably fulfilled.

The picture we find disconcerting is one which portrays the building blocks of matter as particles with well-defined spatial boundaries and separated from their neighbours by relatively vast regions of empty space. Consider for a moment the system on which this picture may be based. How, we may ask, is it possible that the moon, some quarter of a million miles away, can have an influence on the earth's tides? Such action at a distance would appear to place our understanding of causality under strain. At the heart of that conception is the notion of one thing's acting upon another, as when an object is pushed, pulled, cut, twisted, and so forth. When there is no such interaction we are puzzled as to how the causal relation can be realised. Clearly, and rightly, we are thinking of moon and earth as having the spatial boundaries which are given to vision: two roughly spherical objects situated at a considerable distance from one another. But suppose we adopt a different determination of a body's boundaries, thinking of both moon and earth, and any other heavenly body, as existing wherever their gravitational force can be felt. After all, a radio wave may be diffused throughout a wide area of space, being said to be wherever it can be detected. This is, of course, just another way of speaking, in no way at odds with the commonsense scheme, but it delivers a different picture: moon and earth breaking through their visually given boundaries and extending far out into space; far from existing in splendid isolation, as thus envisaged they overlap one another, with no question of action at a distance.

Likewise with subatomic particles. Here too we are free to forego the picture of a sharply delimited boundary which the putative surface would define, putting in its place the idea of a field of force which encompasses both particle and adjoining space, the particle as originally conceived of remaining as a singularity within this more extensive structure. We no longer have a sharp transition from the complete emptiness of space to the substance of a body, but there is a field which, in terms of the forces that define it, is nowhere empty. With the adoption of this picture we 'fill in' the immeasurable tracts of emptinesses that had generated our problem, a problem which is now seen to be the result of an unreflecting acceptance of a simple model.

The shift to this conceptual scheme may make for the removal of our puzzlement, but the very fact that we have this licence surely testifies to the inescapably theoretical character of whatever scheme we adopt. But what does that mean? Not, to be sure, that the facts must be in question. The choice we have been considering is one between different sets of concepts, so, if you wish, between different theories; but 'theoretical' does not in this connexion mean 'conjectural'. Still, it may be said, so long as we are speaking of the unobservable, we shall have to invoke language which makes essential use of models, of extended or transferred uses of language. There will always be this veil between us and reality. I have no doubt that, here as elsewhere, we shall find it useful and natural to employ models, to couch our descriptions in language which makes no claim to literal truth. However, that this *must* be so, even with the unobservable, is far from obvious. Here are two points to consider.

First, it is naturally felt that where direct observation is lacking, theory is the best we can have. The reasoning, presumably, is that only with direct observation are we able finally to rule out competing alternatives, but it is not clear that observation of putative *effects* of a particle might not yield more information. Direct observation – including observation using a microscope – may disclose visual forms to which no particulate structure corresponds, being more akin to painted dots on a continuous surface, whereas the effects may be less ambivalent in what they tell us about such structure. Moreover, when it is said that the entities in question cannot be observed, it is important to ascertain the reason for this impossibility. If it is merely technically difficult, we have an obstacle that may in time be overcome. If it is more than that, if it makes no sense to speak here of observing, then such a lack cannot be grounds for alleging a shortfall or limitation which might perpetuate merely theoretical status.

Second, although a visual aid, as given by the Bohr model of the atom, is valuable, it would seem that we are not at a loss when it comes to giving a literal specification of features of the phenomena in question, but that the prosaic vocabulary of spin, mass, charge and the like, is well suited to just this task. I suspect that what clouds our understanding here is a misconception along the following lines. We can soon be brought to acknowledge that certain categories, as those of colour and texture, have no place in a description of the submicroscopic world which has any claim to unvarnished truth. However, the acknowledged failure of a given category is thought to leave a gap which some other category, as yet unspecified, must fill. But that – the inapplicability of certain categories – is *all* that a critical approach yields; stripping a particle of something it never strictly had does not mean that there is something else in the newly vacated logical space which has now to be tracked down, let alone something which may forever elude us.

*

The other reason mentioned for querying the factual character of our everyday ascriptions of properties to physical things turned on the supposed subjectivity of secondary qualities. We shall briefly discuss this question through the example of colour.

Surveying a flower garden in full bloom, we shall not find the reality of colours difficult to embrace. Indeed, if someone should tell us, 'Nothing is *really* coloured', it would be inappropriate to give the tolerant reply: 'Who knows, you may be right.' As though: we are only fallible; it would be presumptuous to suppose that any of our beliefs, however firmly grounded, could never in any circumstances be overturned. Such tolerance is misplaced, in that, if our beliefs about colour are one and all to be abandoned, then our very understanding of that area of the language deserts us: we simply have no idea what being coloured *means*; we are being denied the use of the kinds of sample in terms of which colour words were explained to us and to which we should in turn appeal with our explanations. There is nothing recondite in our use of 'colour' or of names of particular colours; we do not have to master an abstruse theory before pronouncing something to be coloured, but 'green', say, just is the word we have learned to apply to things like apples, leaves, and so forth, whatever further facts about the colour investigation may turn up. This is not to say that error is inconceivable in a given case. Inspecting a suit under artificial lighting we may pronounce it to be uniformly grey, only recognising our error when, re-examining it in the daylight, we make out a fine pin stripe. But this is a way of going wrong that is brought home to us within experience. The sceptic's denial of colour to the fabric is not a prelude to a triumphant unveiling of a piece of apparatus that has fooled us into taking the opposite view. He is not offering his claim as an *empirical* one.

If it is not an empirical claim, what is it? The sceptic does not expect his experience to follow a different course from anyone else's; on the other hand, it is difficult to see how he could make out a case for saying that our ascriptions of colour are not empirically false so much as unintelligible. All it seems that is left for him is to be *stipulating* how he proposes to use the language. This, clearly, is how it has to be if, say, he maintains that the absence of a causal role for colours makes for their unreality, or if he declares them to be unreal because they do not match up with any physical properties, whether of light or of the surface which reflects it. There is no use of 'unreal' in connexion with colour which would sanction this description, and the proposed use is, of course, not one we need follow. We shall no doubt still wish to identify things by reference to their colours, to point out that the colour of the curtains does not match the sofa; we shall continue to be concerned if someone looks pale, expect the blackened tarts to have an unappealing taste, and so forth. The sceptic can go his own way linguistically if he wishes; so long as he does not suppose there is any good reason for us to go with him.

But might it not be more than a stipulation? Might he not have found a contradiction at the heart of our way of speaking? A concept can be described as useless, unfruitful, or even empty, but not *false*; that belongs with the larger unit, the assertion. What of 'self-contradictory', or 'inconsistent'? Either is possible, but would seem to have no application to colour words, whether the model is that given by an explicit

'*F* and not-*F* ', or whether it is that of a word with more than one meaning, this latter being what talk of inconsistency more commonly amounts to for individual expressions – as with the adjective 'public', which in the phrase 'public school', confusingly means 'private'; not a circumstance which lands us with saying that something both is and is not public, in an objectionable reading of these words. All that is shown by such examples is that the usage of a single word may be such as to confer more than one meaning upon it. English spelling is inconsistent in a similar sense, a single form, such as 'ough', being associated with a variety of sounds. In either case inconsistency means no more than the lack of a single pattern. There is no question of some aspect of the language's being somehow incoherent.

Inconsistency even of this variety is certainly not the rule for colour words, and the considerations cited above show how wrong it would be to condemn these as *useless*. But if the sceptic cannot impugn our ways of speaking here, perhaps he can question the significance of what for us is so assured. It is not for him to query ascriptions of 'yellow' to buttercups, but nothing has been said about what these involve. Might not a deeper analysis of what we unthinkingly accept turn up surprises?

The difficulty here is in determining whether our ways of speaking leave room for any of the possibilities which the sceptic, or indeed any other philosopher, might wish to press. In particular, it would appear that the objectivity of judgements of colour is pre-empted by their grammar: an ascription of colour will do as well as any for purposes of explaining what it is to offer an objective characterisation of something. Thus, what is achieved by improved lighting conditions, or closer proximity to the object, is a better opportunity to see how it stands with the *object* in respect of colour, a failure to discriminate colours pointing to a defect on *our* part.

But, surely, it would not be at all remarkable if a better understanding of the physics and physiology of vision revealed flaws in our commonsense picture. The scientific approach is geared to a conception of the world as it is in itself, independently of any contribution that can be put down to us, with our particular senses and make-up generally. If, in speaking of colour, we are speaking of an end effect which has the character it has thanks in part to that make-up, then there is at least an element of relativity to be acknowledged. But this *if* is not to be granted: there simply is nothing in either mind or body to which 'yellow' need in any sense attach when we see a buttercup; *a fortiori*, there is no question of our 'projecting' onto things something that is strictly within us, but the focus remains resolutely with a feature of something at a distance from us.

The subjective view is often presented as an elaboration of the proposal that being yellow, say, is a matter of looking yellow to normal observers in standard circumstances. This appears to embody a relational conception, and it is congenial to the idea that the world as presented to us in vision is mere appearance. It leaves room for a consistent addition: but it isn't *really* yellow.

However, the notion of how something looks will not do what is asked of it here. First, it is important to see why 'it looks *F*' often has a tentative character, leaving the way open for 'but it isn't really'. This feature is a

41

reflection of the *restricted* scope of such a judgment. In saying that something looks damp, say, we are indicating that our judgment is based only on what is disclosed to sight in the given circumstances, and since what is learned or surmised in this way may not suffice for a final verdict, we leave room for a contradictory judgment. If this is correct, then we should expect any suggestion of uncertainty to be absent so long as there is no call to supplement the findings of vision by those of other senses, or by what might be disclosed to vision on other occasions. And this is indeed what we find with, for instance, such an observation as 'A jukebox looks out of place in a church'. Conceivably we may wish to leave room for 'but it isn't really', but it is at least as likely that 'looks' is chosen simply because the object offends *visually* in those surroundings. Again, consider 'The room looks better with the new wallpaper', where there is little scope for the addition, 'but it isn't really'.

When, now, it is said that being yellow is a matter of looking yellow, the point of 'looks' is to direct us to the visual, rather than to allow room for error or relativity. If it is said that yellow things merely *look* yellow, this can hardly mean: but they're not really. The generality of the claim leaves us with no possibility of specifying any circumstances in which this denial could be substantiated. What we have is simply the platitude that yellow things are only *seen* as yellow. If it is true that buttercups look yellow only to *us*, that is because for some reason we alone are capable of perceiving that colour. That is, we have at best an empirical, not a grammatical, truth. The only relevant 'relativity' having a claim to the latter status is: yellow things are yellow only to *sight*.[8]

2. Fact and Theory

*

Another area which has not escaped the attention of the theorists is that of so-called 'folk psychology', the conception of human beings embodied in the range of everyday psychological concepts which we use in their regard, and in particular which we use when explaining human behaviour. Is this a matter of a *theory* that has become entrenched in our way of thinking, or are we at the level of fact, with nothing to fear from advances in our understanding of human beings from psychology and physiology?

If, observing someone shaking the branches of a tree, you conclude that he is doing this because he thinks he may thereby get some fruit which he wants, then you are enlisting an explanation of the kind in question. The pattern thus illustrated – specifying an end desired along with a belief as to how it might be attained – defines the most familiar form which our explanations of behaviour take. Indeed, literally 'defines': it is a matter of explaining why the person is doing what he is doing in a sense of 'why' which is not addressed when, for instance, physiological springs of movement are being investigated.

This claim stands, of course, in need of justification. First, a few words on the themes which may develop when it is said that terms such as 'desire' and 'belief' belong to a theory of the mind.

One emphasis may be on the possibility of choice: our explanations customarily proceed in the way indicated, but it is possible that other concepts should prove more fruitful. Once more, however, this does not make it appropriate to enlist the term 'theory' in connexion with what we currently have, since the possibility of conceptual choice does not impugn a claim to be stating facts in the language which is actually used. And there is a further caveat: in so far as the explanations which are to employ the new concepts are still to answer the old questions, this has consequences for the range of alternative concepts that might be invoked.

It is in place to speak of theory if we can treat desires and beliefs as explanatory posits or constructs, as hidden mechanisms, a view embodied in the functionalist's conception of them as inner causes which mediate between external stimuli and behaviour. At one time it was believed that emotional and physical dispositions were due to certain bodily fluids – blood, phlegm, choler or yellow bile, melancholy or black bile. To call a person phlegmatic, meaning not simply that he manifested a stolid, unemotional disposition, but that he did so in consequence of the action of the relevant bodily fluid, might be said to be a matter of offering a theory-based description, and would contrast with a use of the word which aimed merely at indicating what could be established without benefit of any causal hypothesis. At first blush, the general run of terms which we enlist in our psychological characterisations appear to conform to the latter pattern, but a more modern causal interpretation is nowadays common ground between most defenders and detractors of folk psychology alike.

For the detractors, the causal role which beliefs and desires supposedly have in explanations of behaviour makes it appropriate to speak of folk psychology not merely as a theory, but as a *bad* theory: neuroscience knows nothing of inner states with the character of a belief or desire to be found among the causal antecedents of behaviour. Not merely that, but once the causal role of beliefs and desires has been discredited, the very rationale for postulating their existence has vanished; they are to be discarded as part of a primitive myth, one which has now outlived any usefulness it may have had.[9] To assess this position we must look at the way causation enters into our conception of the mental.

There are two cases to consider, depending on whether the mental is thought of as cause or as effect. (I am going along with the common philosophical use of 'mental' in respect of sensations and other phenomena for which the classification is in fact questionable.) The latter is the less problematic. Like any other happenings, sensations, emotions, moods, thoughts, and so forth, are presumed to have causes, and it might well be part of an explanation of 'pain', say, that pains are sensations which are typically brought about in a certain fashion. The possibility of the mental itself as cause is less assured; certainly, it would be rash to read into the very definition of a type of sensation an involvement with causation from this direction. Prima facie, there are difficulties with the view that pains are even potential causes, yet for the functionalist a pain is by definition a sensation that is apt for the production of certain forms of behaviour.

Suppose that the grammatical question is settled in favour of the functionalist, at least to the extent of a conclusion that pains *may* be causes. Even with this obstacle surmounted, it remains possible that pains invariably occur at the *end* of a causal chain, that they themselves never initiate anything. Take a typical case which invites a causal construal, as when, touching something very hot, you immediately withdraw

45

your hand. Persuasive though it may seem, this is not an incontrovertible case of pain causing a bodily movement, since it remains possible that sensation and reflex are twin effects of a common cause. Indeed, not merely possible: it is a matter of experience that the recoil is sometimes found to be under way fractionally in advance of the sensation.

If our folk psychology somehow required us to opt for the former possibility, it would be vulnerable, but if the causation in fact follows the latter pattern, then while we can be convicted of error in declaring otherwise, it is simple empirical error. It is not one which somehow brings down our whole way of looking at people and pains, but it is the sort of error which our beliefs generally – and of course our concepts – can survive. Indeed, what the possibility just described shows is simply that the functionalist definition is not true to actual usage – not, regrettably, that there are no pains.

Likewise with other psychological terms. We constantly speak of thinking, hoping, wishing, fearing, and so forth, and cannot contemplate wholesale error and illusion here without renouncing our conception of ourselves as persons: we have not only *Cogito ergo sum*, but if there is never any thought or feeling then there just are no human beings. What an extraordinarily powerful argument it must be that would dispose of so much! But of course there never could be an *argument* – reasoning, inferring, assuming, concluding – any more than there could be illusion or misconception. These are all part of the family of notions which neuroscience has supposedly exposed as mythical.

A rejection of folk psychology which takes this extreme form is plainly incoherent, contradicted at every turn by the practice of those who would make it. And yet it has seemed an inescapable consequence of the causal character of the mental. Let us then consider the explanatory scheme which is seemingly behind this incoherence.

If, speaking honestly, I tell you why I am doing what I am doing, then the reason I make known unquestionably *is* my reason, and cannot be faulted as such. Why am I fiddling with the clock? I am trying to get it to go. Why am I opening the cupboard? I want to see if the teapot is inside. What sense can be made of the suggestion that I may be in error with these explanations? No more, surely, than someone's allegation that you are thinking about Caesar's conquest of Gaul can be accepted in the face of your honest disclaimer that any thoughts on this subject have entered your head. This is not to say that all human behaviour can be explained in this way – it has to be a matter of voluntary action – nor that the agent will always be ready with such an explanation. The claim is merely that when, meaning and understanding what we say, we state our reason for acting, then what we avow does not stand to be defeated by any rival.

Confronted with such a claim, the more promising rejoinder is not to contradict it, but to seek to play down the value of the explanation yielded. After all, there is in general a price to be paid for immunity from error: we can expect the significance of what is said to be in inverse proportion to its invulnerability. Such a charge could perhaps be sustained if a declaration of one's reason purported to be knowledge gained by eliminating possible sources of error, but if it has its significance for what it *shows* about the person, for the

47

state of mind which it manifests, then the objection does not find its mark. What is often of paramount importance to us is a person's state of mind: is he ill- or well-disposed to those who stand to be affected by what he does? An expression of intention or desire can make that plain where a putative claim to knowledge, e.g. about physiology, might well leave us totally in the dark. Again, if someone is engaged in actions which we find opaque, we shall want to know what he takes himself to be doing. He tells us he is rubbing two sticks together to generate a flame. We may be sceptical of the likelihood of success, but at least we now know what he is about, what he thinks he stands to gain from his efforts, and his honest word can enlighten us in a way that probing the workings of his brain would not.

In giving our reason for acting we are not advancing a causal explanation. This contention may seem at odds with everyday usage: when we speak of a *reason*, can we not in many cases speak equally of a *cause*? There is indeed an overlap between the terms, particularly in such phrases as 'gives cause' and 'gives reason', and we can use 'because' with reference to either. However, the corrigibility of causal statements marks out a sense of 'cause' – one at issue when we are considering what requires experimentation to establish – in which it is appropriate to contrast it to 'reason'.

One's reason for acting is, I have argued, as one sincerely declares or acknowledges it to be. Whether or not A caused B, on the other hand, is not a matter for an incorrigible judgment. A's causal role may be thought evident, but this apparent obviousness may simply reflect the salience of A among the cluster of

happenings preceding *B*, further investigation reveal-
ing that, say, the only relation the two enjoy is that of
effects of a common cause. There are psychological
studies documenting cases where subjects have been
in error about the causation of their behaviour.[10] As
long as this is the kind of causation which depends on
investigation, the possibility of error – as with our
example of pain and recoil – can never be excluded,
however unlikely it may strike us.

However, granted that avowals of a reason for action are not open to challenge, so not to be understood
in causal terms, this does not show that reasons are
not causes, only that our concept of a reason does not
require that they should be. The difference revealed, it
could be said, is one in the *concepts* of assigning a cause
to one's movements and giving one's reason for acting.
That is so, but the difference is enough to disallow the
title 'causal explanation' to the explanations in terms
of beliefs and desires. Moreover, the truths which
structure the relevant explanations are grammatical
in character, so in no sense a matter of theory: we may
say that a person who wants to *F* above all else will do
so if he knows he has the opportunity and the ability,
but that is not a behavioural law; it is analytic of
'wanting to *F* above all else'. We possess few, if any,
laws with which to explain behaviour, the explanations we offer frequently resting on 'imponderable'
factors and seldom generalising beyond a narrow
range of cases. If they can be described as 'theoretical'
that can mean only that they are, as often happens,
conjectural, not that they are part of a *theory* of human
behaviour. And of course many of our remarks about
others are not by way of explanations, but simply
reports or descriptions, as of someone grieving, rejoic-

ing, commiserating, confiding, and the like.

The term 'belief', like 'thought', is in one important use not even qualified to name a potential cause, namely, when it admits such qualifications as 'cherished', 'primitive', 'implausible', 'false' and 'shared'. A firm, deeply held, controversial belief is not an internal state of a person, let alone of a person's brain. There is a gross compounding of errors when it is said that beliefs enjoy not only a causal but also a semantic role. It is then quite correct to say that there are no such things as beliefs, thus defined, but the appropriate response should be the more modest one of seeking to see where the analysis has gone astray, not a dismissal of beliefs as unreal. Whether or not another person believes that *p* can, of course, be problematic – another occasion for speaking of conjecture, though hardly of theory, and certainly not of a causal theory. And even conjecture is not inevitable. It will not apply when it is a matter of one's own beliefs, and it is frequently not so with respect to the beliefs of others. A more plausible candidate for cause is belief in the sense of believing, but again, whether or not this is ever a successful candidate, the satisfactoriness of our explanations does not wait upon finding it to be so.

*

The argument of the preceding sections might be thought to depend on an indefensible view that commonsense beliefs are sacrosanct, that they inevitably win out when matched against philosophical theorising. However, where falsity makes sense, I am leaving ample room for it with a judgment of the relevant kind – a judgment about someone's desires or about the colour of something, for instance. It is just that the only way I see these as realistically capable of falsity is as *empirical* judgments. The attempt to find them at fault on conceptual grounds produces at best an alternative grammar.

Now, however, the objection may shift to a challenge to the use made of this contrast. Anyone who is impressed by arguments against the tenability of a distinction between analytic and synthetic propositions will doubtless feel that the division between the factual and the grammatical which I have called upon is ill-conceived, an impression which will not be diminished by the consideration that the range of the grammatical is patently broader than that of the analytic – my reason, indeed, for invoking the former term. We shall now look briefly at the broader class here being opposed to the factual *qua* empirical, but with the viability of the narrower distinction in view.

Suppose we have an equation relating imperial and metric units, say '1 metre = 39.37 inches' (to the first two places). What is the status of such an equality? Is it a logical or merely an empirical truth? Let us assume that this equality is arrived at by applying an imperial measure to the standard metre rod, that the result is obtained by an 'experiment'. Clearly, the experiment is one which could go more than one way, depending, for instance, on the temperature of the rod. None the less, the result, or perhaps one of the results obtained, is singled out and declared the norm, or at least treated in this way. In such a case the equality accepted rests on a convention, a decision.[11] As such, it does not fit easily into the category of logical truths, but while it has a clear affinity with an empirical proposition – it results from taking just such a proposition and converting it into a stipulation – it seems right to oppose it to this, to locate it within an extension of the former category. It is not difficult to think of many mathematical propositions as having arisen in this way. For instance, we accept only those results of addition which respect the integrity of what is counted, setting aside those where, as with drops of water, the items counted coalesce.

Given the possible role for stipulation or convention, it does not seem that non-empirical character makes automatically for status as a logical truth (or falsehood). Consider Einstein's adoption of the convention that light takes the same time going from B to A as it does going from A to B. This is not a symmetry that can be empirically verified, and however strong its appeal to reason, it can hardly lay claim to logical truth. Indeed, alternative conventions can be consistently entertained, even if they appear arbitrary, and result in a more complex mathematics. What is critical is that they are not vulnerable to falsification, even though they lack the sanction of conceptual necessity. The convention is not something secured by the meanings of the terms, but what it does is as it would do if it were the latter: it prescribes an equality amongst measures in a way that does not leave open the possibility of an empirical refutation.

When a proposition has the role of fixing a concept, registering a convention, there is scope for speaking of choice: we could have fixed the concept differently. When we are working against the background of an established usage, of concepts already fixed, there is not *that* source of choice, but only what indeterminacy can offer – which may be little or nothing. When considering the determination of a concept we need not declare a willingness to stay with the proposed usage come what may. Why close the door to what may come to recommend itself as a more fruitful network of conceptual relations? In so far as those who consider a flexible approach to analytic truths the only rational one have something like this in mind, there is a coherent thesis in the offing, but in so far as an established usage is being presupposed, it may not be clear that there is room for choice. Contrast Einstein's equality with the more general rule which governs the relation, namely 'Two magnitudes which are equal to a third are equal to one another'. Again, usage of 'knows' may preclude saying 'A knows that p but it is not so', in which case nothing even counts as 'false knowledge'. Usage may of course not go this way, but to refuse that it may is surely to rule out a genuine empirical possibility on *a priori* grounds. It is of no help in understanding how the excluded form might be made sense of *now* to appeal to the indisputable truth that usage might be different in the future.

The distinction between the analytic and the synthetic is, I am inclined to say, as good as the claim that on one occasion p was used as a rule for testing, whereas on another it was deemed potentially open to empirical disproof, a proposition which might itself be tested. It would seem wrong, that is, to suppose that the tenability of the distinction is at the mercy of a continuing attitude towards a given form of words; in the case of analyticity, that we should forever regard factual considerations as irrelevant to its acceptability. That enduring stance is required only for an enduring ascription of analyticity; a current attribution of that status is not dependent on its future continuation. In other words, I am rejecting the common characterisation of analyticity in terms of immunity to revision. That does not describe the use which we may make of p on a given occasion and which warrants the description as analytic for that occasion, but this is a matter of considering only questions of usage as relevant to truth. Perhaps the usage leaves the status of p indeterminate. That does not dispense someone who advances p from making explicit how his assertion is to be understood, but such clarification is necessary if we are to be sure that any criticisms we offer are to the point. Likewise with propositions of the broader class. Einstein was adamant that in specifying equal time intervals for light signals over equal distances he was making a *stipulation*, not a supposition or hypothesis.[12] And he was right to draw the division so emphatically. Physicists would have had every reason to protest if, asked how he intended his equation, he had confessed himself unable to say, and justified this unhelpful response by citing the lack of a sharp divide between factual and conceptual matters. In so far as anyone is making a serious claim or proposal it is for him to tell us how we are to take it, what that claim or proposal *is*, even if some radical rethinking might at some future date lead to a different approach.

3

Fact and Value

When facts are conceived of as spatio-temporal items, differences in kinds of fact come to be construed as differences in constitution, rather than merely in subject matter. This leads to particular difficulties with certain of the species, notably those answering to negative and general propositions, along with the category which we shall now investigate, that of moral facts. So long as they draw on this misconception, objections to the possibility of such facts need not detain us, but a genuine issue remains in so far as the question whether there are moral facts amounts to asking whether moral issues can be definitively settled. That they cannot is an inference encouraged by the never-endingness of disputes which rage around such issues as the rightness or wrongness of capital punishment or euthanasia. Since it does not seem possible to trace the disagreements to information possessed or anticipated by one party but not the other, it is difficult to see how the disputes might be resolved. Indeed, difficult, it may be said, to regard them as being disputes as to fact at all. More generally, it has been frequently and vigorously contended that there is an unbridgeable gulf between fact and value, moral matters being just a subspecies of the latter category. We shall now attempt to see to what extent this opposition is warranted, an investigation which, we shall find, shows a surprising degree of continuity with the approach of the last chapter in the emphasis to be placed on disentangling factual from grammatical considerations.[13]

Despite the abundance of seemingly intractable moral debates, it is easy to formulate value judgments which would commonly pass as uncontroversial. It is a fact, surely, that divorce is often bad for the children involved. If anything, the complaint might be that this is an understatement: divorce is often *disastrous* for the children. More generally, such judgments have every appearance of constituting a particular variety of factual discourse. Consider: 'She was a kind and gentle person', 'Your cousin cheats at cards', and 'His books tend to be unimaginative and poorly written'. The grammar of these propositions is very much that of an attribution of a style of behaviour or a property to someone or something; they are all propositions which we have no hesitation, in favourable circumstances, in pronouncing true or false – to such a point that it may become difficult to allow that one who sincerely dissents can share our understanding of them. What could we make of a person who thought it a good thing to be cold, wet, miserable and lonely; fed up, deeply in debt, frightened out of one's wits and bitten by a rabid dog? Surely, his position could be taken seriously only if he explained that, however unexpectedly, there was something to be gained from this state of affairs that was as clear a case of a good as these are, prima facie, instances of the undesirable. It is proper to contradict another in regard to such propositions, to ask for evidence, to seek to identify something through the information they purportedly offer, to be truthful or untruthful in giving voice to them, and so forth. In short, their grammar, and usage generally, do not favour an exclusion from the class of informative, descriptive discourse.

Here is a further consideration. The claim that moral issues are inherently contentious must take into account the extent to which disagreements are traceable to differences in non-moral beliefs. The believer and the non-believer, for instance, may have conflicting moral views, but the non-believer may concede that if he shared his opponent's religious position then his own moral code would fall into line with his opponent's. Again, a person who is confident that 'pain' and 'suffering' apply as straightforwardly to animals as they do to human beings is likely to be more ready with moral judgments relating to the treatment of animals than someone who does not share this confidence. Likewise with political convictions. We might argue against a socialist utopia, not on the grounds that the state of affairs envisaged is not desirable, but because we believe that only an exceedingly gullible person could think that human beings could be brought to behave in the requisite way. Once more, the parties in dispute might find their differences resolved if they saw eye to eye on their expectations of their fellow men. On any view of moral language we should expect there to be perennial debates; inflate the numbers by including those which rest on differences in non-moral beliefs and the impression is readily given that values are in another realm altogether from facts.

How are value judgments to be characterised? On the other side of the divide we have a reasonably workable starting point: with a purely factual or descriptive term, w, to know the meaning of w is to know how things have to be for w to apply to a person or thing. On the value side the choice is greater, embracing notions which bring in a reference to the language-user – expressing a preference, a feeling, a pro- or con-attitude, guiding choices, prescribing, commending and condemning – along with such notions as those of goodness, badness and obligation, which an ascription of value may be thought to imply. To arrive at a proper appreciation of evaluative language we might start with the descriptive scheme and see how, if at all, it needs to be supplemented. After all, the extent of that scheme's applicability should not be underrated, even with 'good' and 'bad' the obvious focus being on how things stand with the objects or behaviour to which they are applied. The most influential and sophisticated view which finds the scheme wanting is the prescriptivism advocated by R.M. Hare, and we shall make this the main focus of our enquiry.[14]

Hare's position is usefully approached through the earlier 'open question' argument put forward by G.E. Moore in trying to show what is distinctive of goodness. According to Moore, no matter what characterisation is proposed by way of elucidation of this notion, we can always meaningfully raise the question whether something which satisfies the characterisation really is good. If, for instance, it is suggested that 'good' means 'conducive to the general happiness', we can coherently retort, 'I agree that x is conducive to the general happiness, but is it really good?' The eternal possibility of such questioning shows goodness to be, Moore thought, a species of unanalysable, non-natural property.[15]

If we set aside Moore's conception of properties and definitions – not favoured with a large following nowadays – the general approach is clearly seen to be flawed. The supposedly open question would come to grief if the language had a synonym for 'good', and indeed the question is firmly closed when a term such as 'perfect' or 'excellent' is invoked. Hare's advance was to formulate a more substantive issue by imposing a necessary restriction on the kind of definition of 'good' which might more plausibly be held to leave the question open. According to Hare, what is characteristic of this and other value terms is their *prescriptive* use, their use in guiding choices (to take one of the principal characterisations). The connexion thereby made with practice, with action, is absent from purely *descriptive* language, language used merely for saying how things are. Armed with this distinction, we can reformulate Moore's open question as follows: no matter how something x is *described*, it always makes sense to ask whether x, thus described, is really good. The gap between fact and value is understood in terms of a gap between two significantly different uses of language. In particular, the use characteristic of 'good', and which sets it apart from purely descriptive language, is a use to *commend*. Two people could be in complete agreement on every descriptive detail of the universe, yet not agree whether a state of affairs was good or not, divergence on this point being possible precisely because a preparedness to commend the states of affairs specified lies quite outside that specification.

The immediate predecessor of prescriptivism was the emotive theory of ethics, which saw the distinctive feature of value judgments in a use to express and evoke feelings. In the face of the frequent lack of passion of those engaged in such exercises as grading apples or appraising athletic performances, not to mention judging of past or hypothetical actions, this approach became difficult to sustain. Prescriptivism avoids the crudities of emotivism while siding with that approach to the extent of leaving room for an essential contribution from the language-user, one involving his attitudes, feelings, intentions, or whatever. However, the resultant analysis has not been considered above criticism. To call something good may be to commend it – though often it is not – but what of those numerous uses of the word in which nothing is actually *called* good – where, for instance, it is asked or doubted whether something is good?[16] Deciding that *x* is good is surely not a matter of deciding to commend *x*, let alone deciding that one does so. True, while such a paraphrase is questionable, we can maintain a role for *calling good* in such contexts by replacing 'is good' by 'is to be called good' or 'is what is called good'. Such a proposition as 'I doubt that this is a good bargain' then becomes 'I doubt that this is what would be called a good bargain'. However, it might reasonably be countered that this just highlights the underlying difficulty in another way. The suggested paraphrase is acceptable if it comes to something like 'I doubt that this has what it takes to be (called) a good bargain', but if there is, as it were, no constraint on the side of the article to which 'good' is being applied, then the mere fact that it might be called good is of diminished interest. I have no doubt that this would be called a good bargain by many, but that just shows how easily people can be taken in. We should like to know whether it has what it takes to merit this epithet, whether it is *justifiably* called good.

This reflection accords with another natural response to a prescriptivist analysis. If a word allows of incorporation in a use of the relevant kind – as to commend, condemn, advise, warn, or in other ways guide choices and influence behaviour – this will be because of its character at another level, the level, precisely, of meaning as explained through the descriptive scheme. The capacity of 'That is hot (electrified, poisonous)' to be enlisted in warning someone is dependent on the word's drawing attention to a certain property of the thing in question. This speech act exploits a feature of the word which is constant whether or not one of the prescriptive uses in question is also present. Likewise with 'good': it is because it means what it means that it is so useful for purposes of commending. We need not challenge the ubiquity of the prescriptive use, but it is parasitic on the purely descriptive character of the term.

But surely, if we thought that 'good' was essentially descriptive, we should be unable to make sense of its use with respect to things as descriptively diverse as pianos, pens and policemen. With a prescriptive function to appeal to, by contrast, we are not without the resources for identifying a common strand to the word's uses: despite the diversity of the persons and things, 'good' has a unitary role in commending them.

But consider the phrase, 'has what you are looking for'. These words do not alter in meaning as they are used, now in connexion with a piano, let us say, now in connexion with a pen, but they operate at a sufficiently high level of generality to be associated with features particular to pianos in one application, and with features particular to pens in another. Moreover, the phrase combines two other interesting features: it can be incorporated in judgments which clearly qualify as factual, and it can be used in guiding choices.

61

Indeed, it is rather better for guiding choices than is 'good'. If you are trying to decide which among objects of a given kind to select, being told that such-and-such is a good one is useful, but since your particular interest and purposes may not be those which people generally have in the class of items in question, you will be more concerned to know which of the objects meets your own requirements.

The phrase 'has what you are looking for' was not singled out by accident to make these points, but it is clearly a close relation of 'good' itself.[17] It may be held that to explain what makes for a good F it is often not necessary to look beyond F itself to any connexion with desires or the like, but x is a good F to the extent that it has what it takes simply to be an F, or is every bit an F, as with a good likeness or a good three miles. In many such cases, being in no way lacking as an F means being effective as an F – a good push, a good talking to – or being in some other way as we want an F to be – a good friend, a good climate – so perhaps a link with desire is never lost sight of entirely. At all events, whether or not this class is always included, it seems we can often capture the sense of the term with some such phrase as 'has what is wanted in things of that kind', where, unlike 'has what you are looking for', only the general desire or interest is alluded to. Once more such a phrase can be ranged alongside those appropriately classified as descriptive; it may differ from many of these in its level of generality, but that is no disqualification. On the other hand, its generality adequately explains why a new lesson in the meaning of 'good' is not required each time we extend the term to a new class of objects.

If 'good' can be rendered along the lines of such a

paraphrase, we can readily explain both how it can single things out on a descriptive basis and at the same time be well suited to a role in guiding choices. It is clear that we retain the idea of an object judged good as thereby being presumed to be one way rather than another, as on the descriptive scheme, and the idea of a commendatory use as relying on this implication.

But judgments of goodness can seldom be counted upon to meet with universal assent. How is this to be explained? There are two likely ways in which disagreement may arise. First, unqualified judgments of goodness are silent on the question of whose or what interests are involved, often requiring relativisation to the relevant parties and purposes if they are to present a well-defined issue. You learn that you hold the winning ticket in a lottery. Good news or not? There is no place for a judgment of goodness independently of all relevant interests, but it may be possible to say without qualification: good news for you, not so good for me. Second, there is is the possibility of variation in the standards adopted, one person – or generation – demanding more than another of a given object before pronouncing it good. So, what is today reckoned a good computer will doubtless be thought quite primitive in a few years. When technological advances make it possible to ask for more of a given artifact, our demands, and our ascriptions of goodness, will alter accordingly. Differences in standards undeniably make for different assessments of goodness, but without forcing a retreat from the descriptive scheme; like 'what is now wanted', 'good' contains the variability needed to accommodate these shifts.

*

We shall pick up goodness again shortly, but first let us broaden the discussion. 'Good', after all, is only one among a vast number of value terms. Although the speaker's point of view may be crucial for a judgment of goodness, in the majority of cases a more general or typical interest must be met for the use of the word to be justified. What holds here also holds for a large class of words associated with feelings, as 'boring', 'irritating', 'pleasing', 'shocking', 'fascinating', 'amusing', and so forth. As befits their grammatical character – adjectives derived from transitive verbs – these terms direct us to an *effect* which something thus describable may have on someone. However, what may not be clear from their use, but the source of disputes, is the range of that effect. Consider 'boring'. A description of a novel, say, as boring is likely to reflect at least the speaker's reaction, the impact the novel had on him, and in so far as no further qualification is introduced, the suggestion is that this is not simply an idiosyncratic reaction. A novel may bore some, it may engross others. If it is reasonable for the speaker to suppose that his own reactions are not atypical, to that extent it is reasonable for him to use the impersonal form. That form, however, stands to be refuted by the verdict of others. Whatever he may think, if others find the novel quite absorbing he has no right to the unqualified judgment first ventured, but is obliged to retreat to something like 'Well, *I* found it boring'. Often, of course, there will be an unspoken restriction to a certain subclass of potential readers. One could happily acknowledge that the bulk of mankind should find the novel boring through incomprehension of the language, but not feel it necessary to defer to that reaction, since one's audience would not be thinking of these wider reactions as providing a form of falsification which proceeded on a basis of sufficient interest or relevance to be worth taking into account.

Needless to say, there is considerable indeterminacy in such a term, but what is important to note is what it relates to, namely the matter of the range of people presumed to react in the relevant way in order for the description to be warranted. The relation to value is no more critical to this feature than it is with 'puzzling' or 'exhausting'. Moreover, when a feature of value is at issue there is no escaping the possibility of falsification by appeal to such involvement, but due regard being made for their undoubted indeterminacy, appraisals of something as boring stand or fall accordingly as people are or are not affected in the requisite way. This is often resisted, especially with such words as 'disgusting', 'appalling', 'shocking' and 'revolting', which some may persist in invoking even when it is obvious to them that they are in a minority, that in their mouths the words are no more than expressions of personal distaste. Such a person is likely to round on dissenters with the claim that they *ought* to be disgusted, appalled, shocked, or revolted, but whatever we think of that, it is a different issue, and does nothing to vindicate the use of the impersonal formulation. It is also clear that such judgments are unlikely to enjoy any lasting validity: jokes which our forefathers found amusing may draw no such response from us, and matters which shock us may leave our children quite unmoved.

When it is said that moral judgments express feelings, so are not to be assessed as true or false, we may be puzzled by this supposed consequence. Why should such a judgment, so construed, not be true when the feelings are as affirmed? Just such a point is what we have been arguing with respect to the analogous class of words expressive of the kinds of reactions instanced. Their relational character makes for an interesting variation on the descriptive scheme, but not for its abandonment; reference to individuals affected is at the heart of these words' use, but not in such a way that it offers the slightest challenge to the claim that the object is being credited with a certain capacity. Moreover, the logic found with this particular grammatical form is more widely applicable, similar observations being apt with 'funny', 'enjoyable', 'outrageous', 'attractive', 'easy', 'tedious', and so forth. The implicitly relational character of a judgment that a setting is attractive is consistent with its objectivity, in the sense that there is no error in referring the property of being attractive to the setting, no cause to say that, in reality, we are merely projecting something in us onto the world. There is again a natural tendency to give a dominant place to one's own reactions when appraising something in these terms, but that may be simply to indulge in rhetoric, to misuse such language rather than to respect the essentially impersonal logic which their unqualified use demands.

We have seen how phrases which come close in sense to 'good' can have a meaning which is to be elucidated in purely descriptive terms, yet be apt for a prescriptive use; indeed, be apt precisely because of their meaning. A large number of words may be reckoned value words on a somewhat weaker basis: they do not import an essential reference to a desire or attitude, but they simply signify a quality or trait on which we commonly place some value. So 'lefthanded' and 'retired' do not specify features for which we value those thus described, whereas 'polite', 'witty', 'punctual' and 'sympathetic' engage with favoured traits, 'arrogant', 'superficial', 'inconsiderate' and 'conceited' with traits commonly found objectionable. Other terms, such as 'expensive', 'distracting' and 'strict', may enjoy either status. In some circumstances the observation that an article is expensive may be intended as a criticism; in other circumstances it may be thought to constitute a recommendation, in yet others it may be entirely neutral. The explanation of meaning proceeds identically in all three cases, the commendatory or critical uses being extra to anything which use in accordance with the word's meaning demands. When the word is commonly associated with a single attitude it will often be difficult to see how a person could not find the trait in question of positive (negative) value, but it would still seem right to characterise the term as one which applies to a feature that is generally held in favour (disfavour), rather than regard sympathy with the attitude as a precondition for a correct use of the word.

I say that 'arrogant', say, is a value word just in the sense that it picks out an aspect of character which we value negatively. Two objections are likely. First, it may be insisted that there is an implicit judgment of badness or undesirability in ascriptions of arrogance. Second, it may be said that if no such judgment is implicit, it is none the less in some such terms that the substantive issue is to be presented. On the first point, it would seem that there are many terms which have nothing stronger than a customary connexion with a positive or negative evaluation, and that it is important to allow that they can reasonably be reckoned value terms none the less. It is important, since it is not infrequently supposed that character as a value word is at odds with having well-defined criteria of application. On the second point, we have still to consider some of the terms which might be thought to convey the evaluative dimension, but, in so far as 'good' provides the model, we have as yet no grounds for thinking that this dimension will not be a further function of their descriptive meaning. Here it is worth noting that with 'boring', for instance, we are speaking of an effect that is perforce disliked, so attracts a negative evaluation, but it is merely the range of persons supposedly affected that makes for a problem in knowing whether a bare description as boring is warranted; no further problem is posed by the inevitably pejorative character of the description.

The sense in which the words so far considered may be said to express an attitude is in most cases somewhat roundabout. Consider 'cheat' and 'liar'. These would often be classified as 'emotive' words; certainly, to call someone a cheat or a liar is to invoke strong language. However, while the strength of such language may well be a reflection of the strength of feeling, the degree of disapproval, which people commonly have towards those whom they consider deserving of these descriptions, it would not seem that this attitude has to be shared by someone who seriously ventures characterisations of a person in such terms. If, on hearing you say that Smith is a liar, I conclude that you are not well-disposed towards him, there are two likely bases for my conclusion. First, given the distress and inconvenience which those who lie are prone to cause, and the almost universal dislike or disapproval of such behaviour, it is not unreasonable to assume that this widespread attitude is one you share. Second, knowing that this is the general attitude, a person will be aware that in drawing attention to this trait he may well influence the reactions of others to the person thus described, so he is unlikely to make public what he knows or believes in this respect unless he takes a dim view of the behaviour in question, so is prepared to see the person fall out of favour with others as a result of his making known this aspect of his character. That a condemnatory use of the words is secondary is made abundantly clear by the following consideration. Condemning, like commending, is a step we may take *further* to having a given moral belief, a step which comes with making that belief known. I may be led to the unavoidable conclusion that an acquaintance is a liar, but merely to have drawn this conclusion is not so far to have condemned him. For that a public declaration of my belief is necessary. Likewise, my commending of something as good is logically secondary to my having made up my mind as to its character. This style of argument brings out the derivative status of the favoured speech acts, though it also shows that there is a sense in which an evaluation cannot be logically derived from a factual premise: as a performance, an utterance of the relevant words cannot be derived from anything at all.

The descriptive scheme is standing up well, but it might be thought to have no bearing on terms of endearment and abuse which involve likening the recipient to someone or something liked or disliked, as with 'angel', 'honey', 'scum' and 'pig'. Since there is no question of a person's having literally what it takes to be described as a pig, it may seem that there is room for a semantic role very different from that enjoyed by words whose correct use requires answering traits on the part of the person to whom they are applied – the pattern found with factual discourse. Is not 'pig' in this connexion *just* a term of abuse, a term relating to something coming from the speaker rather than to something to be found on the side of the abused?

Given that literal application is ruled out, this alternative looks appealing: factual identification has weakened to the point that we are left with nothing more than an emotive element, an expression of dislike or disgust. However, even with a term such as 'pig' we retain something of the idea that the subject of this characterisation is made out to be of a certain character. Indeed, it is generally a matter of a specific form of supposedly disagreeable behaviour – odious eating habits rather than, say, insincerity. The question then becomes the now familiar one as to the extent of the reaction to the behaviour, as with 'disgusting'. Terms which relate to bad behaviour are in turn not interchangeable with those which relate to foolishness, and even within these categories we can find distinctions on the side of the behaviour or persons described. Consider the differences between 'idiot', 'ignoramus', 'nitwit' and 'oaf'.

What is true, and a possible source of misconceived support for the anti-descriptivist, is that words in this class present a high degree of indeterminacy. And not only in this class. Less figurative vocabulary will also be affected by a measure of indeterminacy which may make for differences in judgment from person to person. It is not laid down just how large a donation has to be to qualify as generous, for instance, how full of himself someone has to be to count as conceited. However, not only does this not mean that there are no clear cases, but, once more, it is a matter of a more pervasive feature of language, telling us nothing about specifically evaluative words. Consider measures of quantity, as 'vast', 'diminutive', or 'protracted'. When these are connected with value we may have a motive for exploiting their ill-defined character, but such character is theirs independently of any such connexion. Or again, take the term 'difficult'. This may be associated with value, but that is an incidental feature of its use, very much secondary to the feature which accounts for the variability in judgments of what is difficult. That feature is simply that we are not at one in what we find difficult.

*

So far we have found nothing which points to a general exclusion of matters of value from the sphere of fact, but the features which may defeat a clear verdict on a value judgment are features to which descriptive language at large is prey – uses of words which involve some figure of speech, or a degree of vagueness or indeterminacy which leaves us without anything sufficiently well-defined to be settled as true or false. Certainly, there is nothing to be gained from looking to prescriptivism to find what is distinctive of evaluative language. However, there is more to be said on what makes for differences in moral outlook, and we shall now rejoin our discussion of goodness to pursue this topic.

If you and I have tickets in the same lottery and yours wins, the result will be good news for you, not so good for me. Here it may seem fruitless to argue the question of goodness without specifying for whom the result might be good. On the other hand, once such specification is provided, the resulting statement of goodness may be incontrovertible. But whatever is said of this example, there will be cases where an overall assessment is just what is sought. So, a proposed road may be clearly in the interests of those who wish to travel between the towns which it will link, but it may equally clearly not be a good to those along the route whose peace will be shattered. Two relativised judgments which both parties may endorse, but that is not where the problem lies. We wish to know whether overall, all parties considered, the road will be a good thing.

It is at this point that the utilitarian has something to say. For him – or for most adherents of utilitarianism – the course of action to be pursued is the one which, as far as possible, maximises happiness or utility. As offering guidance on such a substantive point, it is not surprising that this moral code comes in for criticism. Here a general observation is worth making. Objections raised against utilitarianism may take two forms: they may purport to reveal flaws in the theory, but they may also point to difficulties with which the theory has to grapple, but which are to be classed as difficulties presented by a troublesome reality rather than failings in any moral theory which takes them seriously. We shall now consider two examples of difficulties which are mistakenly presented as being of the first type when they belong with the second. The topic is important, since once more it draws attention to non-moral matters which may lie behind moral differences.

First, the need for the utilitarian to take into account the consequences of actions may be thought to disclose a weakness at the heart of his position. For any given act – the assassination of Kennedy, let us say – there would appear to be no question of saying whether or not it was good, given that its consequences may be felt indefinitely into the future. Even on Judgment Day we shall not be in a position to make an overall assessment of goodness, since for this we should have to know what would have happened had the event not taken place, and this is quite beyond any calculation.

But what are we to infer? That it is pointless even to try to work out the consequences of the various alternatives open to one? Surely not. We know that if we drive carelessly we risk the lives of other road-users. It is true that a death or injury for which we are responsible may turn out to have unexpected advantages which outweigh the loss or suffering, but it would be rash to make that possibility the basis of our behaviour. What is abundantly clear is that the immediate consequences of dangerous driving stand a significant chance of being bad, and it is this, what can be assessed as likely, that provides the basis for a rational decision.

Second, a common objection to the utilitarian is that it is impossible to carry out his necessary assessments of happiness and unhappiness. The diverse forms of both may be incommensurable, the assignment of numerical values may be quite arbitrary, and so forth. It is certainly easy to think of circumstances in which we should be hard-pressed to weigh up alternatives as required and arrive at a satisfactory overall assessment. The question once more is what we are to take this to show. Suppose you have the task of entertaining a number of children on a rainy afternoon. You can think of various pursuits which will keep some happy, but none which do not have attendant disadvantages. Perhaps the younger ones can be kept out of mischief only at the cost of boring the older children; perhaps there is every likelihood that the more popular games will end in tears for some or damage to the surroundings. You may heartily agree that your task is beset with difficulties, but that does not dispense you from doing your best to reach a solution. The anti-utilitarian critic cannot be saying that the rational procedure is simply to abandon any such calculations. One thing, after all, may be clear: if you throw up your hands in despair and simply do nothing, disaster is sure to follow. Likewise when more momentous choices are contemplated, as with the apportioning of public funds. There may be no definitively superior way of allocating money to health, education, defence, and so forth, but it is clear that some procedures would be hopeless – giving everything to education, let us say – so this provides a starting point which we can only improve upon.

Severe though they are, these difficulties are to be seen as real difficulties, not difficulties which arise only for a misconceived theory, but it is also clear that, along with the practical problem, the problem of organising something which will go some way to pleasing everyone, we are faced with the need to make sense of a comparison between disparate consequences, and with this we become embroiled in a *grammatical* issue. We shall now look further at this aspect, since it is a source of disagreement which is not always seen for what it is.

The utilitarian seeks to maximise happiness, but there will typically be more than one course of action that can be thought of as in conformity with that aim, given the different principles on which happiness may be measured and distributed – measured both within its various forms and in relation to unhappiness. An interesting possibility is given with Wittgenstein's observation: 'The whole planet can suffer no greater torment than a *single* soul.'[18] So, apparently, you cannot 'add up' unhappiness across individuals, but the maximum amount of unhappiness at a given time is limited to the amount suffered by the most unhappy person. A more explicit endorsement of this view is found in an attempt by C.S. Lewis to soften the objection to the existence of an all-powerful and benevolent deity presented by the existence of suffering:

> We must never make the problem of pain worse than it is by vague talk about the 'unimaginable sum of human misery' ... . There is no such thing as a sum of suffering, for no one suffers it. When we have reached the maximum that a single person can suffer, we have, no doubt, reached something very horrible, but we have reached all the suffering there ever can be in the universe. The addition of a million fellow-sufferers adds no more pain.[19]

Here a principle is in effect being proposed for weighing up or quantifying pain or unhappiness. Despite possible first appearances, it is a grammatical rather than an ethical principle. Or if it is the latter, it is also the former. You may be happy to opt for this scheme, or you may wish to adopt a different system of reckoning, one which deals in running totals to which each new victim of suffering can make a significant contribution, whatever the degree of his unhappiness. Is there a matter of right or wrong here? There is no right or wrong in the answers yielded by the two methods, provided they are correct in their own terms. The respective rules *define* different senses of 'maximum amount of suffering'.

Compare the analogous examples of alternative systems of reckoning in non-moral contexts, as with Wittgenstein's merchants who sell wood at a price proportionate to the area covered by a pile, irrespective of its height.[20] This is not to be dismissed as incorrect if it makes no claim to assign the same price only to piles having the same volume. If for some reason that consideration is of no interest to the merchants, we may be unable to persuade them of the virtues of our own approach. On the other hand, we might well wish to be able to show them that there is something which it would be worth their while taking into account and to which their scheme does not do justice. Similarly, while we may have to grant that a given Wittgenstein/Lewis judgment comparing states of unhappiness is correct in its own terms, few would be happy, I imagine, to leave the matter there. And, indeed, there is plainly a sense in which unhappiness can be said to increase with any increase in the number of unhappy people.

Must it also be acknowledged that such an increase in unhappiness makes for a *worse* state of affairs? Do our concepts settle that for us, or are we left with a choice? Mill's attempt to show that happiness is the sole desirable end is often held to rest on a mistaken analogy between 'desirable', which means 'ought to be desired', and 'visible', which means 'able to be seen'. Whatever we think of this, we might ask: is it really a serious question whether happiness is desirable? Or whether unhappiness is undesirable? These relations have nothing to fear from charges that they involve the naturalistic fallacy, but in so far as there is a difficulty it lies with the claim that happiness is the *sole* good desirable, any way of demonstrating this beyond doubt being inevitably, it would seem, a way of rendering it vacuous.

Notwithstanding this objection, we may sympathise with the utilitarian's project of ordering actions in terms of the happiness they produce and mapping the result onto a scale of desirability or goodness. Roughly speaking, he is saying: the more happiness the better. And this, together with the converse form for unhappiness, seems acceptable whether we are considering the Wittgenstein/Lewis measure, or one where more unhappiness is a matter of more unhappy people. But, needless to say, difficulties remain. First, supposing that this latter way of summing unhappiness is accepted, how are we to choose between major unhappiness for a few as against minor unhappiness for many? The difficulty is familiar enough. My point in mentioning it is simply to draw attention to its essentially conceptual character: how are we to choose, given that we appear to have exhausted the possibilities of the relevant concepts? It seems we can only repeat our relativised judgments – the former distribution is better for the majority, not for an unfortunate minority. The determination of overall badness in terms of overall unhappiness offers no basis for adjudicating between the two distributions, and since overall badness is, at another level, just what we are trying to decide, it is not clear that there can be an answer.

Second, however we reckon overall (un)happiness,

there is a problem in relating the associated scale of goodness and badness to the 'absolute' notions given by *right* and *wrong*. We should often be prepared to say that x would be a better course of action than y, backing this with a higher rating of x in terms of happiness, but not consider it a matter of any seriousness if y were chosen. Likewise, we often say that x is something a person ought to do, but meaning no more than that it would be a good idea to act in that way. In neither case need there be any implication that it would be wrong not so to act.

It is, then, one thing to accept that the scale of good-better-best can be mapped onto a scale of degrees of overall happiness; it is another matter altogether to impose a further right/wrong division on either scale. Some may, it is true, speak of degrees of wrongness, but even if A is said to be less wrong than B, still it is being held to *be* wrong, and where in our scale of goodness and badness, happiness and unhappiness, are we to draw a line such that an act below that line produces so much unhappiness that it can be considered wrong, whereas anything above that line can be reckoned permissible?

In presenting the principle of utility Mill does not answer this question, but we are given only a basis for making comparative judgments with 'right' and 'wrong', much as if he had used the terms which more readily allow of this use, namely 'good' and 'bad':

> The creed which accepts as the foundation of morals, Utility, or the Greatest Happiness Principle, holds that actions are right in proportion as they tend to promote happiness, wrong as they tend to produce the reverse of happiness.[21]

3. Fact and Value

If Mill's form of utilitarianism falters with this equation, another variant, endorsed by Bentham, may meet with dissent on another point which falls within the grammar of the system. According to this version our duty is to perform whatever is highest on the scale of happiness-producing actions.[22] Setting what ought to be done at this point is not arbitrary, in so far as it fastens upon a unique point on that scale, but it is important to see that its standing is only that of a stipulation: we are being invited to accept a counsel of perfection, a counsel which results in the devaluation of lesser acts which would normally be reckoned on the side of *right* rather than *wrong*. You kindly offer to mow a neighbour's lawn. You would no doubt have been the bringer of even greater happiness had you weeded his flowerbeds as well, but you might well feel you had already gone beyond the call of neighbourly duty with your first offer. Or again, it may not be felt that we have any obligation to make contented people yet happier, an observation which also applies to the characterisation of the right action as one in accordance with a law which, if generally followed, would lead to a maximisation of happiness. Clearly it is the conceptual move, the acceptance of the proposed usage, that is critical. That one can, having taken this step, claim the wrongness of a lesser act as fact is then correct, but it does not mean that the issue has been resolved once and for all in favour of utilitarianism.

Both the proposals considered for the right/wrong distinction are easily resisted. What then remains? Could we perhaps correlate degrees of wrongness with degrees of unhappiness, harm, or the like, but say that an action was morally wrong or impermissible when it made for *serious* harm or unhappiness, when its consequences were *very* bad in these terms? That, after all, is pretty much how we do make the division. Take an activity which may affect others in varying degrees, e.g. teasing. This often induces unhappiness, but if minor and fleeting it may be considered of no consequence; if lasting and major, the matter becomes one of moral concern. What should we lose if we took this as the model generally for moral prohibitions and permissions?

Whether or not it would be a loss, it is clear that we should part company with conceptions of wrongness which tie this notion to that of violating a moral law, where the law has that status, not necessarily because of any connexion with (un)happiness, but because it has been laid down by the appropriate authority – by God, perhaps. It is not unnatural to think that in the absence of a divine law-maker, anything goes, or at least that such notions as right and wrong are inextricably bound up with a lawlike system of ethics, that we have no business making use of them if we do not accept this framework.[23] A more modest inference would be, not that the notions of right and wrong make sense only against the background of such a system, but that the only sense we can make of these notions once that background has been rejected is in terms of the notion of serious harm. True, it may be objected that the concept of serious harm is intolerably vague, a likely source of unresolvable disputes. But then it may be an illusion that there is any well-founded alternative to an ill-defined scale of goodness and badness. This may not be a scheme which satisfies everyone, but we are deluding ourselves if the alternatives involve drawing a sharp line where none exists.

3. Fact and Value

Compare talk about moral rights. With legal rights we know more or less where we stand. If you are wondering whether you have a right to return faulty goods you can find out by consulting the relevant legislation. But suppose rights are claimed when there is no authoritative body which confers them. For instance, travellers to outer space lay claim to parts of some distant planet, though without coming under the jurisdiction of any authority which lays down who has what rights in such circumstances. Then a claim to a right looks like so much empty rhetoric – as indeed is frequently the case closer to home: every worker has an inalienable right to two tea breaks a day. The term lends itself well to such exploitation, precisely because it has the role of a clincher in moral argument – get the opposition to concede that you have a right, and you have won your case – but it is possible that the framework which would give sense to such an appeal is wanting. Nor is that framework supplied by calling upon the notion of a *natural* right. The term 'natural' is invoked when a qualification which, like 'legal', would give substance to the notion, is inapplicable. It marks the lack of any such qualification, rather than itself furnishing one.

This is, of course, nothing more than the sketch of argument. What matters is essentially the kind of possibility illustrated – one where we might say that a concept is being misapplied, where conditions for making sense of its application have not been fulfilled. There is yet again no question of rejecting a concept as false, but there is the equally crippling defect of inapplicability. And, of course, without rejecting the concept, we could take exception to the reasoning on which the judgment involving it is based. As such an example, consider the retributivist's insistence that wrongdoing calls for punishment irrespective of the consequences thereof in terms of utilitarian benefits, as reform and deterrence. In his eyes the balance has to be redressed by inflicting comparable suffering on the perpetrator, whereas for the non-retributivist this is a recipe for adding to evil. To refute the retributivist we might seek to convict him of 'arithmetical' error: one evil does not cancel another, it doubles it. He has simply turned his back on the reality of the guilty party's suffering. Or so we might hope to argue. The difficulty here is to distinguish between a different grammar and a faulty application of the same grammar.

Our discussion of fact and theory suggested that the sceptic about perceptual judgments is not going to win out if he tries to discredit these in their own terms – as empirical propositions – but he must either find fault with the concepts used, or explain to us the virtues of an alternative conceptual framework. In this instance, it is difficult to see how the relevant concepts might be challenged, but in the case of moral questions there is more that is open. As well as such obvious sources of disputes as vagueness, indeterminacy, and conflicting interests, we have concepts whose usefulness rests on assumptions which may not be conceded. It may seem utterly obvious that considerations of a grammatical character should come into focus when we are concerned with different moral views: exclude differences as to matters of empirical fact, and what else is left? However, what is obvious here gets overlooked simply because it is thought that we already have a satisfactory answer along prescriptivist lines. The root of the problem is not a gulf

3. Fact and Value

between fact and value; rather, the difficulties divide between the factual and the conceptual: it is often practically impossible to reconcile conflicting interests, to please everybody; it is often conceptually impossible to make well-defined comparisons, in terms of, e.g., desirability, between different actions or states of affairs.

Notes

1. Bertrand Russell, 'The Philosophy of Logical Atomism', in *Essays in Logic and Knowledge*, ed. R.C. Marsh, London, Allen & Unwin, 1956, p. 182. In more recent times, the main defence of facts as worldly items has been advanced by J.L. Austin. Cf. his 'Truth' and 'Unfair to Facts', in *Philosophical Papers*, ed. J.O. Urmson and G.J. Warnock, Oxford, Clarendon Press, 3rd edn, 1979. Austin's position is criticized by P.F. Strawson in 'Truth', *Logico-Linguistic Papers*, London, Methuen, 1971. The present analysis is pursued at greater length in my *Grammar in Philosophy*, Oxford, Clarendon Press, 1979, §§39-42.

2. These misgivings regarding theory, especially in connexion with the 'theory' of meaning, are developed further in *Grammar in Philosophy* and in my *Wittgenstein and Contemporary Philosophy of Language*, Oxford, Blackwell, 1990.

3. Karl Popper, *The Logic of Scientific Discovery*, London, Hutchinson, revised edn, 1968, p. 423.

4. Karl Popper, *Conjectures and Refutations*, London, Routledge & Kegan Paul, 3rd revised edn, 1969, p. 118.

5. N.R. Hanson, *Patterns of Discovery*, Cambridge, University Press, 1965, p. 17.

6. The claim that our perceptual judgments go beyond the evidence for them, and that material objects are to be introduced as posits, is to be found in A.J. Ayer, *The Central Problems of Philosophy*, London, Weidenfeld & Nicolson, 1973, chs 4 and 5.

7. Arthur Eddington, *The Nature of the Physical World*, London, Collins, 1928, p. 9.

8. For a thorough investigation of this issue see P.M.S. Hacker, *Appearance and Reality*, Oxford, Blackwell, 1987.

9. Essays devoted to this topic are to be found in J.D. Greenwood, ed., *The Future of Folk Psychology*, Cambridge

University Press, 1991.

10. Cf. Richard E. Nisbett and Timothy DeCamp Wilson, 'Telling more than we can know: Verbal reports on mental processes', *Psychological Review*, vol. 84, 1977.

11. Cf. G.P. Baker and P.M.S. Hacker, *Wittgenstein: Rules, Grammar and Necessity*, Oxford, Blackwell, 1985, p. 326.

12. Albert Einstein, *Relativity: The Special and the General Theory*, London, Methuen, 1920, p. 23.

13. The following discussion is based on my 'Disputes and Values', in *The Business of Reason*, ed. J.J. MacIntosh and S.C. Coval, London, Routledge & Kegan Paul, 1969.

14. R.M. Hare, *The Language of Morals*, Oxford, Clarendon Press, 1952.

15. G.E. Moore, *Principia Ethica*, Cambridge University Press, 1903, ch. I.

16. Cf. J.R. Searle, 'Meaning and Speech Acts', *Philosophical Review*, vol. LXXI, 1962.

17. Compare Paul Ziff's definition of 'good' as 'answering to certain interests', in his *Semantic Analysis*, Ithaca, Cornell University Press, 1960, ch. VI.

18. L. Wittgenstein, *Culture and Value*, ed. G.H. von Wright in collaboration with H. Nyman, tr. P. Winch, Oxford, Blackwell, 1980, p. 46.

19. C.S. Lewis, *The Problem of Pain*, London, Collins, 1957, pp. 103-4.

20. *Wittgenstein's Lectures on the Foundations of Mathematics, Cambridge 1939*, ed. C. Diamond, Sussex, Harvester Press, 1976, p. 202.

21. John Stuart Mill, *Utilitarianism*, Everyman's Library, London, Dent, 1910, ch. II.

22. Jeremy Bentham, *An Introduction to the Principles of Morals and Legislation*, ed. J.H. Burns and H.L.A. Hart, London, Athlone Press, 1970, p. 14.

23. Cf. G.E.M. Anscombe, 'Modern Moral Philosophy', in *Ethics, Religion and Politics*, Oxford, Blackwell, 1981.

Index

also available in the Interpretations series

LAWS OF NATURE

Rom Harré

Fellow of Linacre College, Oxford

The laws of nature, on which all science is based, are supposed to have three characteristics: to be supported by evidence, to be universally applicable, and to enable us to predict what will always happen in the same circumstances. In this book a philosopher of science examines some of the well-known laws of nature from the point of view of all three characteristics. He shows that science is possible only within a metaphysical framework, a general assumption of the existence of natural kinds. The idea is used to explicate the scope and modality of laws of nature and also to resolve some of the classical paradoxes which have emerged when they are studied in the light of their logical form alone.

ISBN 0 7156 2464 4

also available in the Interpretations series

PARADOXES

Justin Leiber

Professor of Philosophy at the University of
Houston, Texas

Paradoxes are many things. Artificial intelligence
views them as viruses of the brain, strange replicators
that unexpectedly exploit design possibilities. For the
child, they are intellectual cartwheels, an everyday
delight. For mathematicians and logicians, they reveal skeletons in the closet of reason. For philosophers
and dramatists, they capture the contradictions of
experience. The historian of ideas sees that they come
in successive waves, surging through Classical
Greece, the Renaissance and the twentieth century.

Professor Leiber's user-friendly guide to paradoxes
provides an up-to-date survey of an ancient and perennial source of puzzlement.

ISBN 0 7156 2426 1

also available from Duckworth

MIND MATTERS

Series editor: Judith Hughes

Many philosophy books claim to be written for the general reader as well as the academic, but all too few really cater for their needs. This series explores philosophical issues and is written specifically for the general reader.

Each book starts with the kind of question we may ask ourselves without, perhaps, realising that we are 'philosophising'. Do computers have minds? Can a pile of bricks be a work of art? Should we hold pathological killers responsible for their crimes? These questions are explored and new questions raised with frequent reference to the views of the major philosophers.

The books in the 'Mind Matters' series are concise, lively, inexpensive, jargon-free and, above all, a fascinating read.

ART OR BUNK?
Ian Ground

For many people, the infamous pile of bricks in the Tate Gallery, Carl André's *Equivalent VIII*, is still the most potent symbol of modern art, and it is what inspires Ian Ground's question 'Art or Bunk?' Using his wide knowledge of classical aesthetics and current ideas in the philosophy of art, he guides us through various attempts to say just what sort of thing a work of art is, and shows us a way to answer the question. Although his examples relate to the visual arts, his arguments are applicable to arts in general, and his book provides a much-needed lively and readable introduction to aesthetics.

Hbk ISBN 1-85399-014-0 £17.95
Pbk ISBN 1-85399-015-9 £6.95

BEFORE EUREKA
the presocratics and their science
Robin Waterfield

What kind of science and scientific thinking went on in the West before the familiar names of Aristotle and Archimedes claimed centre stage? Actually an extraordinary amount – extraordinary both in volume and in breadth of scale. Their enterprise was no less than to describe and explain the whole universe and all its major constituent parts. Their achievement was to establish the authenticity of the rational human mind as a tool for tackling the universe in a matter-of-fact manner.

Robin Waterfield not only describes the Presocratic enterprise in a clear and lively way, he also questions what science is, and whether the Presocratics were scientists in the modern sense of the word. As his previous publications range from the sublimity of Greek philosophy to the fantasy of children's space-age fiction, he is well qualified to write this book.

Hbk ISBN 1-85399-074-4 £17.95
Pbk ISBN 1-85399-075-2 £6.95

CAN'T WE MAKE MORAL JUDGEMENTS?
Mary Midgley

How many times do we hear the statement, 'It's not for me to judge'? It conveys one of the most popular ideas of our time: that to make judgements of others is essentially wrong. But doesn't this idea itself involve a moral judgement? What is it? Could we possibly avoid making it? Why have so many thinkers urged us to do this impossible thing?

In this lively and approachable discussion, Mary Midgley turns a spotlight on the fashionable view that we no longer need or use moral judgements. Guiding the reader through the diverse approaches to the complex subject, she points out the strong confident beliefs about such things as the value of freedom that underlie our supposed scepticism about values. She shows how the question of whether or not we can make moral judgements must inevitably affect our attitudes not only to the law and its institutions, but also to events that occur in our daily lives, and suggests that mistrust of moral judgement may be making life even harder for us than it would be otherwise.

Pbk ISBN 1-85399-166-X £6.95

Mind Matters series

DOES GOD EXIST?
Mark Corner

Do people talking about God know what they are talking about? Are they all talking about the same thing? How do different religions approach the existence of God? Can God's existence be proved? And even if it can, is God necessarily good?

Does God Exist? sets out to provide a lively and readable introduction to the main issues of theism and atheism. The author takes a fresh look at the question that has always been at the very roots of philosophy. His arguments provoke further interest as a source of new ideas.

Pbk ISBN 1-85399-164-3 £6.95

DO WE HAVE FREE WILL?
Mark Thornton

'Do We Have Free Will?' is not just an abstract philosophical question. It shapes educational and legal theory, it underlies particular views in Sociology and Psychology, and it is apparent in decisions in social and political policy.

Mark Thornton has produced a comprehensive guide to the rich variety of philosophical opinion on the subject. His clear exposition, penetrating criticism and original suggestions make this a valuable book for anyone with a practical or theoretical concern with issues of human freedom and responsibility.

Hbk ISBN 1-85399-018-3 £17.95
Pbk ISBN 1-85399-019-1 £6.95

MAD OR BAD?
Michael Bavidge

Michael Bavidge's question, 'Mad or Bad?' arises out of a long-standing philosophical interest in the connections between ethics and the philosophy of mind and from surprise at the verdicts in some notorious murder trials. Dreadful crimes demand total, unreserved condemnation and heavy punishment, but their very dreadfulness also leads us to think, 'Anyone who does *that* must be mad!'

This book provides a thought-provoking and sensitive new attempt to show us how we can preserve our ordinary moral intuitions about dreadful crimes while facing up to the difficulties of holding psychopathic criminals fully responsible for their actions. It is an important topic with wide-ranging implications which affect us all.

Hbk ISBN 1-85399-016-7 £17.95
Pbk ISBN 1-85399-017-5 £6.95

MINDS, BRAINS AND MACHINES
Geoffrey Brown

Whether or not machines can think is the stuff of which dreams and nightmares are made. Geoffrey Brown lives in this world, however, and his expertise in computer engineering gives him a down-to-earth view of the present complexity and future possibilities of the machines which appear to control much of our lives.

But he is also a philosopher who sees that the question demands careful consideration of some fundamental issues. What do we mean by 'think'? Is machine 'thinking' like human 'thinking'? What does it mean to be conscious? And in answering these questions we reach the heart of what is called the philosophy of mind.

Hbk ISBN 1-85399-012-4 £17.95
Pbk ISBN 1-85399-013-2 £6.95

REASONABLE CARE
Grant Gillett

If any discipline poses questions of life and death it is medical ethics. Where the availability of treatment is limited, who should get priority? Should doctors force treatment on unwilling patients? How can we judge whether a life is worth living and who should decide? *Reasonable Care* helps us approach these questions by offering a survey and critique of contemporary medical ethics, but it does so by drawing heavily on actual practice and the problems faced by doctors, nurses and their patients.

Grant Gillett is ideally placed to straddle the philosophical and the practical worlds, because when he is not writing and teaching philosophy he spends his time doing neurosurgery.

Hbk ISBN 1-85399-072-8 £17.95
Pbk ISBN 1-85399-073-6 £6.95